The Purple Rose

and Other Essays

TIM DALGLEISH

The Purple Rose and Other Essays

Copyright © Tim Dalgleish 2017

Cover photo Tim Dalgleish

Published by Tim Dalgleish, Createspace Independent Publishing

ISBN 1545105162

ISBN 9781545105160

Dedicated

to

Mum

for making Zealandia worth living in

CONTENTS

ALSO BY TIM DALGLEISH

Non-Fiction

Scotland before Scotland

Lifting it off the Page

The Guerilla Philosopher

Playing Macbeth: An Actor's Journey into the Role

Poetry

Reflections from Mirror City (anthology)

The Stones of Mithras

Penumbra

Plays

The Last Days of Adam

Gormenghast (with Carabosse Theatre)

Fragile Fire (with Voices of the Holocaust Theatre)

The Life and Theatre of Antonin Artaud

The Collector (with Caz Tricks)

Editor

The Rose by WB Yeats

Dracula's Guest by Bram Stoker

The Ballad of Reading Gaol with Humanitad by Oscar Wilde

After Dunkirk by Major John Dalgleish

Wilde, Yeats, Stoker: Great Writers of Ireland

Preface

The title of this volume of essays, the first of two, refers to the first essay in this collection and my first beginnings as a writer. The second strand of my life has been acting and that explains the cover photograph. That's me in the air. I'm in a children's play called *Princess,* on a nationwide tour, which finished at the Edinburgh Festival Fringe. I don't think I've ever been as high again.

The general feature that connects most of the essays in this volume is that they are largely autobiographical. That being the case it seemed the best place to start was with a couple of essays that refer to events and subject matter from my early life.

Roughly speaking, the first eight essays continue chronologically until we return to childhood with the essay *Industrial Valentine.* The next seven essays from *Volcano Theatre and Nascent Writing* to the fragment of a play called *Ted Hughes Meets Sylvia Plath* are more or less directly about the theatre. The last ten essays contain the biggest mix of subjects (and perhaps writing style) with essays on God, ghosts, friends, film and Being.

The essays have been ordered so that if one reads the book from start to finish the subject matter is mildly interconnected and shorter essays have been placed in between longer pieces to break things up and provide a little variety.

However, I know that, for many readers, half the fun of reading a book of essays is that they can pick and choose what they want to read based on which titles on the contents page seem most appealing. This is a perfectly reasonable approach to this collection, as the essays were written over a long time span, for a host of different reasons and are not intrinsically connected to one another.

Finally, some of the essays are prefaced with a short introduction, in italics, to contextualize what follows. Just to confuse matters, however, the opening essay happens to begin with a quote (not an introductory paragraph) and so is in   italics.

The Purple Rose of Juvenilia

What You Write When You Want to be a Writer

'I needed to write the greatest piece of literature ever written. To have all those dusty crowding hordes of so many years, borne and grafted onto the white hot sparkles, cast out, by the furnace of just expounded ideas. Then, them flung shakily to the crest of almost founded belief, causing shimmering ripples that were snubbed onto paper. To have blanket type piles, of slide upon slide of flashing emerald and vermillion images, flow, inspirationally inked. Upon and within, to create a safe island of leather bound permanence, a heavy gold-leafed masterpiece.

Truly was I a poet. A human, dueling mighty vipers to wedge open jaws of unperceived kingdoms; clutching uniqueness. For a rewarding life, I knew, the toxic spirit, pleasure (poetry's essence) must never master work, the cleansed blood of living. Pleasure must create work.'

These were the first words I ever wrote as a writer. What one might correctly call the purple prose of juvenilia.

I had written poems before this of course and even a few pages of story but only at the behest of school teachers. This was the first time I had consciously written 'as a writer', as someone who wanted to be an author.

Typed onto, not quite uniform, A4 sized, blank cream-coloured paper, my first attempt didn't go any further than these two florid sub-Nietzschean paragraphs. That is, until the next attempt, again typed and covering a single sheaf of paper, with *'1B'* handwritten in the top right-hand corner. This specimen had the same opening paragraph, with fewer typos, and then continued:

My knuckles coloured white as I clenched my fingers, 'The grass in the garden needs cutting (to a conventional length).' This was my waking thought. My arms hoisted, buried veins of green

4

tracked traces of ruby over the backwood of my pale hands. God what a day.

I was truly a poet. A human of unique potential, dueling mighty vipers to wedge open jaws of unperceived kingdoms, grasping and clutching the abyss. For a rewarding life I knew the toxic spirit pleasure (poetry's essence) must never master work, the cleansed blood of living. Pleasure must create work.

I was alone with the morning dust...'

It goes on for a few more paragraphs then peters out. Another later version includes the paragraph:

'Man has shown that poets live ever in the agony of life, never fulfilled till their work is complete and never complete till the sun crosses sadly below the mauve horizon. At length questions leather with use. Now and then, instinctively, time is the only question.'

Portentous stuff. Version four or five increases the grandiloquence:

> *'I was an author.'* [Obviously I was settling into the role] *'I wanted to write literature, a great sculptured block of granite permanence thrust into the valley of art. Stuck, and to be no longer modern, once I had fallen. So when written, my soul was to be buried, my body however had to die. Of course it was romantic rubbish and all the garbage I spewed the first day I threw out. But it was a start.'*

Behind the hyperbole is hidden the boy I once was, the exaggerated metaphors and overblown aspiration, reflecting what I felt was inner destiny.

It might appear that I was over ambitious or worse arrogant, as I wrote of writing, *'the **greatest** piece of literature ever written'*. That would be a misjudgment however, one that ignored the palimpsest of folly that represents most people's juvenile self.

The opening line is more tempered than it might at first seem. Its first words, *'I needed to write…'* are not definitely saying that the writer *will* write, *'the greatest piece of writing ever written'* rather that he *needed* to. In those golden days of innocence I was full of love for the idea that perhaps I could write. I had an overwhelming and absolute, if gentle, dream.

I imagined the joy of writing, of burning brightly and being possessed by *Art*. I wanted to describe the world and being alive in a way that other people felt was revelatory, emotionally powerful and caught something of the ethereality our existence.

I still do. I am still pursuing that dream. I think Robert Browning was musing on such life-dreams when he wrote, *'Ah, but a man's reach should exceed his grasp, or what's a heaven for?'*

Perhaps I should be embarrassed by these early fumblings but I can't find it in myself to be. They never grew into a story (though I wrote a dozen versions). There was no story. I was more concerned with the idea of *being* a writer than with actually working out *how* to write.

This disparate chain of words was like a necklace, broken by the awkward trowel thrusts of an inexperienced archaeologist, lost before it was even unearthed. Even so, this first discovery still glimmers with small shards of truth. They don't hold together quite but I can day-dream of how they might've come out with a defter hand.

Even today I half believe, '...*poets live ever in the agony of life*' and I still don't see that as a depressing statement. The melancholy drifting up from the pages of a writer or poet is a comfort (for reader and writer alike). This melancholia is a quilt of infinite pattern, an elemental blanket of warmth, against the winters of life.

Melancholia, via Old French and Latin, comes to us from the Greek *Melankholia*. *Melan-* meaning 'black' and *-kholē* meaning 'bile'. This darkness is what frequently prompts the writer to write in the first place.

When Philip Larkin wrote in *This Be The Verse*,

'They fuck you up your mum and dad'

Sure, he felt 'fucked up' but he wrote the line in *sympathy* with his parents, following it with,

> *'They may not mean to, but they do…*
>
> *But they were fucked up in their turn'.*

There is a bile and blackness in his words but it is the blackness that reveals the light.

Heavyweight Debut

I have included the very short review that follows simply because it was the first piece of writing I ever had published.

To this day I can recall the excitement I felt; the breathless anticipation at the prospect of seeing my words in print. I actually composed the review overnight, whilst lying sleeplessly in bed at the Dickens' house (the Dickens's being a family that our family were friends with). This was necessary due to the fact that the deadline - how amazing to have a deadline! - was for the next morning.

It was Colin's mum, Ann Dickens, I seem to recall, who had somehow arranged for me to be the reviewer for the Bedfordshire Journal, on Thursday, May 16th, 1985.

Ampthill's new heavy rock band, *Tobias*, played their first live gig at Redborne School on

Thursday.

Six months preparation went into the show which also raised money for multiple sclerosis.

'Fun was our main aim' said drummer Colin Dickens. Other members of *Tobias* are vocalist Ian Veary, lead guitarist Mick Veary, Dave Smith on keyboards and Justin Time on bass.

Once warmed up with the hard and harsh song, *Bitch*, the audience was rocked through, *The Gates of Heaven* and later rolled - slightly more gently – through such songs as *Sarah* and *You're Gone*.

Their string of ten original songs ended powerfully with *It's Got To Be Rock n' Roll.*

The Comics of Childhood

This morning I was reading the early chapters of the autobiography of Graham Greene. In it, he was talking about the things he read when he was a child, mostly he was talking of books but he also mentioned a particular comic. This put me in mind of my own experiences growing up. I was not, as I am now, much of a book reader in my early teens but I did devour comics.

By the nineteen-seventies, the real era of popularity for comics was, with its once stalwart standards, such as *The Wizard*, *The Eagle* and *Boy's Weekly*, long gone. I think, even as a youngster, I knew this kind of thing was a bit 'old hat'. It's true there were other kids I knew who bought comics but not regularly or consistently, nor with any depth of passion. Comics were, I felt, my own half-secret pleasure.

The first comic I recall buying on a regular basis was a now long forgotten title called

Krazy. *Krazy* was I now realize with adult eyes, very imitative of previous generations of comic but back then, in my world, it was the bees-knees: new, fresh and exciting.

I bought every weekly edition of *Krazy* for a couple of years (which was, it turns out, its entire lifespan). At some point came an off-shoot brother publication, entitled *Cheeky*, which for a while I bought with equal dedication. *Cheeky* was not, in my opinion, as good as *Krazy* (it's hard to shift that first love) but it was still amusing and contained the exploits of one of *Krazy's* central characters, the eponymous, Cheeky.

The covers were colourful and garish. I loved the smell of the print; the ink; the rough paper. The illustrations, bold line-drawings, were similar to those of *The Beano* and *The Dandy* and all that *Bash Street Kids'* stuff. But to my young mind infinitely more dynamic and up to date. Cheeky had goofy teeth, sticky-out ears and an old man's hair, close-cropped with a few strands projecting out front. He wore a red and black striped jumper, with a yellow 'C' on its front, aping, I now assume, Dennis the Menace.

There was an air, especially in *Krazy*, of jokiness, even one might say, zaniness (very glancingly reminiscence of the lampooning and satirical *MAD Magazine*, which, much later as a teenager, I would go onto enjoy but could never find often enough to become addicted to).

There was a general enjoyment of visual detail and puns, so, for instance, the back-cover was often mocked-up to look like the cover of something else, like a diary, so one could disguise one's reading habits. Most of the rest of the content, additional characters and their storylines and so on, have vanished. They have, like Cheeky in a scrape, slipped away down a drainpipe, the drainpipe of memory that is.

What I am really grateful for and what I gained from this innocent, early, readerly occupation was a certain bibliophilia. I unconsciously grew, absorbed, then developed a love for building and maintaining a library. I could never bear to discard or throw out my weekly purchases and learnt the value or gentle delight, at least, of being able to handle, refer to and organize printed matter.

Naturally, as I grew older, the plots, if one could call them that, and the stories of *Krazy* and *Cheeky* must have begun to seem too facile; too simple. When it first landed on newsagents shelves, in 1977, I recall swiftly switching my allegiance to *2000AD*.

There must have been a crossover period - as *Krazy* appeared in 1976 and ran until 1978 and *Cheeky* ran from late 1977 until early 1980 - but I don't recall this. In memory, it was a clean break from the decidedly childish to the dystopic visions of Megacities and robot wars.

With *2000AD*, literally and metaphorically, there was a whole new literary realm, a (future) world, to experience and explore. Once again the first issue drew you in with a free gift, a red, plastic Frisbee (of sorts) but labelled a 'space spinner' and the front page included the intriguing tagline, *'8p earth money'*.

Ironically, given its supposedly sci-fi futuristic appeal, this first edition included two storylines that harked back to the past. The first was *The New Dan Dare*. The character of Dan Dare being from the nineteen-fifties comic *The Eagle*. The second story was *M.A.C.H.1,* an obvious rip-off (even to my young eyes) of the TV series, *The Six Million Dollar Man* about a 'bionic' superman (which had been around since 1974).

2000AD would greatly improve and become increasingly original in both its illustrations and content. Aimed at an older teenage audience, its central character, the harsh and summarily violent, Judge Dredd, would eventually and unsurprisingly go on to get his own comic.

Judge Dredd has indeed become a minor cultural icon. I always liked Dredd but I preferred *2000AD* as a complete package and have never really been overly interested in the full-colour versions of *Judge Dredd* as a comic or graphic novel. Dredd, like many of the DC Comic characters, has crossed over into film but with perhaps less success than his rival North American superheroes.

My naive thoughts about and experience of

comics was, I imagine, similar to many other young boys and girls of my age and not very dissimilar to previous generations and their experiences. Cartoons, newspaper comic strips and satirical illustrations (such as those in *Punch* magazine which first appeared in 1841) have a very long tradition but comics or comic books began to be really popular with children in Britain in the 1920's and 1930's. *The Gem* and *The Magnet* being a couple of the more famous titles and Billy Bunter, from the latter, is a prime example of character progressing and taking on a life outside his original publication. Bunter appeared in novels, stage plays and eventually on television, in a series which ran on the BBC from 1952 to 1961.

Bunter was created and continuously illustrated and written by Charles Hamilton under the pen name of Frank Richards (one of his numerous non de plumes). It was 'Frank Richards' whom, George Orwell famously declared in his essay *Boys Weeklies*, could not be a single author as the Bunter stories had been running for so long (*The Magnet* ran from 1908-1940).

Charles Hamilton wrote a long letter to *Horizon* magazine (where the essay originally appeared) refuting this and Orwell's other various and numerous inaccuracies. It's reckoned that Hamilton wrote something in the order of a hundred million words during his career, so perhaps Orwell might be forgiven his error on multiple authorship at least. It's certainly surprising to learn of Hamilton's singular industry in a trade in which 'inheriting' a character and then passing them on to the next author is often the norm.

I now have a large library of books which is an endless delight and education. My comics, sadly, I no longer have. For quite a number of years, I had bought, saved and stored many hundreds of comics. At some point, they had, because of their ever increasing voluminousness, been stored in the loft of my family home.

Unfortunately, one year, a few weeks before we moved house, unbeknownst to me, my sister had dutifully ascended into the loft, put all the comics in black sacks and thrown them out. I returned home horrified when I realized my prized collection had vanished. It has been a (gentle) bone of contention between us ever since!

Even now, on wet Tuesday afternoons, thirty-five years later, I occasionally rue that day. In my mind, I have half-seriously vowed - if I have a windfall of a few thousand pounds perhaps – that I will, equally dutifully, buy up complete collections of those comics.

In more sober, less romantic moments, I realize it's something I will never do. Not because with enough time, money and persistence it's not possible. I'm sure, in the age of the internet, one could do a pretty good job of tracking down most, if not all, of the editions of any particular comic that one wanted.

The truth is that having bought a couple of volumes of the collected *2000AD,* as you now easily can, it soon becomes apparent you can't return to those early imaginings, sensations, and delights. The stories and characters have, like the paper, they were originally printed on, faded. You cannot capture the odd, *once in a lifetime*, magic.

All of it seems, at worst, dull, derivative, trite; imitative of very stale over used models and well-trodden, clichéd paths. Cardboard cut-outs have replaced the splendid, funny, diverting, odd, dynamic and stimulating characters that you once invested so much in.

At best, for a moment or two, you experience a 'something', a mental 'aroma' but this is blown rapidly into intangibility as the arid dust and desiccation of the word and image in front of you rises up off the page. The present, real and visceral excitement of going to the corner shop and getting that week's new edition has with the rest of one's childhood, vanished. *C'est la vie. N'est-ce pas?*

The Poetics of Space

Islands and Cities

Not long ago I listened to the BBC Radio 4 programme *Desert Island Discs*. The 'stranded' guest, choosing her favourite discs for the island, was a children's author whose central character, in a series of stories, was a little girl who was herself an islander.

I was in the kitchen doing mundane chores, sweeping, cleaning, washing up and so on and not listening very closely. Not infrequently, standing scrubbing the dishes, my mind wanders, especially with the sound of the radio washing over me.

So 'cast adrift' myself, as it were, my tangential musing eventually came to land at Gaston Bachelard's, *The Poetics of Space*. This is a beautiful and philosophical book on the deep mystery of how we are affected by different spaces. Along with human-made space (or the 'built environment' as architects call it) there is the landscape, seascapes and even the sky, of course, with its multitude of effects, depending on one's location, the time of day and what season it happens to be.

Bachelard is most famous for his idea of 'epistemological obstacles' or 'breaks'. He talked of the discontinuous nature of the sciences, that is, that the history of science being not one of continual progression but rather made up paradigms shifts with new theories being integrated into old but in the process, the sense of the conceptual terms used being altered or shifted.

Bachelard suggested that the fixed mental patterns of scientists, if unrecognized, could become the obstacles to scientific progress and that their psychological outlook and their experience needed to be taken into account.

Mulling on Bachelard made me think of how our physicality, our 'bodied' elemental selves, partially defines our mental existence. The senses communicate an outer place and help (if that's the right word) shape our inner selves, sometimes very clearly, often so distantly we can hardly trace the influence.

We all experience and fill particular spaces with emotion and memory. Bachelard was keen to encourage architects to keep this in mind when creating buildings. He felt the architect should be less driven by the theoretical and abstract reasonings of their field than by potential experiences to be had in the 'made' space. The architect should always put how someone would experience the created space at the heart of their work.

The spaces of contemporary city living, the vast buildings, noisy open plan offices, the sea of people weaving in and out of each other on the street, the warm crush in the underground etcetera. All this, can refine one's separateness, though in *opposition* to the place one inhabits. When the poetics of space are ignored, city life, busy with other people and their projections of identity, can certainly crowd in upon you, take the oxygen you need to think and identify yourself.

The reality of being cast away on the natural space of a desert island may similarly invoke feelings and awareness not simply of isolation but also of how existentially *individual* one is, this manner of solitary existence literally giving one the space to see and envisage the self as an island. In contrast to John Donne's notion that, *'No man is an island'*, I would say, if we are (spatially) beyond the influence of other human beings, perhaps philosophically we are faced more immediately with our cosmic, infinitudinal loneliness?

Island life makes you fold over your thoughts, again and again, a mental origami. In the breeze you have to constantly scribble and rewrite your identity upon the surfaces and fresh pages of inner thought with the ink of the external, the elemental and in the unquiet silence of nature.

Standing alone on our desert island we look out to sea. The sea, the great communicator and creator of self-communication, which echoes, rolls and pushes back, absorbs and stands in for eternity; and the cosmic vastness.

The children's author, mentioned above, had the habit of moving back and forth, from the mainland, to a favourite island. Stimulating and alternately causing her to contemplate, I imagine, the various internal and external spaces, the waves, the white standards of her ever changing self; and like a battered treasure chest, whatever creativity, she found washed to shore.

Cornish Rock and Water God

We were staying for a few days, in a friend's flat, on the outskirts of Porth and walked one morning to Trevelgue Head, one of a series of beautiful headlands along the northern coast of Cornwall. The week before we arrived, the shops on the front, at nearby Fistral, had had their wood and steel walkways ripped down in a storm as if come from an angry god.

It was a bright, cold, gusty, blue-skied morning. We'd wrapped up in waterproofs, scarves, hats and gloves. The last, so as we could use our binoculars, with which we were now watching the various types of seagull dive and catch fish, when, from nowhere, we saw massive clouds of sea spray fired up into the air.

Like comic book ghosts, huge white sheets of water appeared suddenly and then drifted slowly through the air of the coastal inlet below us. The beauty of this, along with the blustering wind and crashing waves, took our breath away.

Peering over the cliff edge we could see that the incoming tide was pushing seawater into a cave or large crevice. After a couple of seconds, the seawater would shoot out in a great plume of white with a grumbling thunder, as if the Cornish rock were awakening, roaring, choking and spewing angrily.

One realized how easy it would be to make a god of this type of event. It was as if the earth had spoken in a loud, tremendous voice, saying, *'Listen, I am here. I am power.'*

A short time later, having moved to get a better view of exactly how this volume of water was being projected and spewed aloft (so forcefully the blankets of spray were caught on the wind), we again stood amazed, as the air borne water passed through, and highlighted, the arc of a rainbow.

It was magical. The sea rushing in, the water filling the cave, a moaning boom, then a massive spume of white, which then met with, and revealed, the ethereal, momentary, streaks of diaphanous colour.

I could have invented a deity from this natural phenomena right then and there. A god whom you crossed at your peril. An awesome, angry, impetuous, heavenly creature, who had wandered heaven and earth, and decided to grumpily settle in these rocks, hoping for peace from both gods and humans. If you disturbed him you'd better have good reason.

Perhaps, now, in the peaceful aftermath of the recent storm, the shop keepers at Fistral should not only repair their walkways and shopfronts but erect a small statue to this god's honour? Keep him happy and perhaps the Cornish rocks will protect; and the water defenses will ward off, the raging sea, next time.

Jack's Problem with Hitchcock

The Trouble With Harry is a well-crafted comic piece of writing by English writer Jack Trevor Story. It's a memorable and amusing novella and also perhaps the best thing Jack Trevor Story ever wrote.

In truth, I haven't read (or at least finished) much else by him over the years because I've always felt his work was a little overwrought, over colourful and just straining too hard - he was a prolific writer and wrote many of the most prized novels in the Sexton Blake Library series, along with numerous film and television scripts. *Harry,* however, is a very precise little book. It is set in the woods and outskirts of a small English town and concerns itself with various modes of eccentricity and the quaintness of murder.

For this very reason, when Alfred Hitchcock made the movie of it, with Shirley MacLaine and John Forsythe in the lead roles and transposed the setting to Vermont, it was always unlikely to work and it doesn't much, although it is a little eccentric.

I suspect this was a novel Jack just 'threw' off and never thought about all that much, except to complain of, and grouse about how little he'd been paid for the rights. Michael Moorcock, in the introduction to a new edition of the book, explains that Hitchcock promised a better deal for Jack on his *next* book, which 'Hitch' then conspicuously failed to film. Moorcock, rightly in my opinion, argues the novella is *considerably subtler than the film* and praises Jack for his celebration of life and his delight in *'the strangeness of ordinary people.'*

I knew Jack, briefly, when I worked for a local history museum in Buckinghamshire and he, believe it or not, lived on the premises. Only half pulling his friend's leg, Jack once told Moorcock that he, *'lived over a stable as part of the permanent exhibit of the Rural Museum'.*

In this period of decline, I would pass him in the courtyard (of what was indeed the old farm house) and he was invariably unshaven, bleary eyed and looking hung-over. Moorcock, obviously a longtime friend and affectionate mate, reports that Jack went on to have a nervous breakdown and even lived rough for a while.

I was working as a cataloguer in the museum and it must have been around the time of 'Glasnost' in the USSR, that is, during the mid-nineteen eighties, because he once asked me how to spell 'Perestroika'. Apart from this stray enquiry, I don't recall much else of what we talked about. Though I do wish I'd had more chats with him because he was a great raconteur and had obviously put a lot of colour into his and other people's life.

He had three wives – as far as he could tell – eight children and a thousand tall stories about his sexual and literary exploits. Many of the stories ended up in the column he wrote in *The Guardian* which ran for many years.

What with his knack for going out with women much younger than himself and his general philandering - much of which, I now suspect, was more imagined than real - I was quite judgmental about him back then (as the poem I wrote about him at the time, and reproduce below, reflects).

Fortunately, he died exactly where he should have, at his desk. He'd returned to health (and his flat) in Milton Keynes but eventually, at aged seventy-four, he'd had a fatal heart attack. He had literally just typed *'The End'* to his last novel, which he'd told his friends was his masterpiece, the autobiographical *Shabby Weddings*.

He certainly left a lasting impression. For me, as someone aspiring to be a writer, that impression was the living embodiment of an archetype: the down trodden, underpaid and underappreciated man of letters. He was not quite the Grub Street hack, more the over industrious, sometimes inspired, wordsmith. As happy-go-lucky, as he was cynical, and as exuberant and cheerful one moment, as he was world weary the next.

Meeting Jack Trevor Story

Facial skin hung in sanguine excess,
Capillaries patched each cheek bone,
With crumpled lip and unclear eye,
A spiky moustache supported his nose.
The face a gnarled, oaken gray,
Teeth chipped, crook, yellow.
He grinned a grin,
The flavour of girls.
The rest was shapeless,
A general haggard stumbling.
Gait, as amorphous as his words,
For the young woman,
But sex was buried in their sound.
Letters, his life, Hitchcock's theft, swapping his
wife, 'What's the meaning of *Glasnost*?' he
asked.
He came to stay in the museum one summer,
A red brick farmhouse, geese, wine, quiet, if he
needed it.
His novels neglected, used,
Bruised and withered,
He said,
Like his own private parts.

Is Chess the Most Boring or Interesting Game in the World?

When I was growing up I used to play chess. I don't recall how I learnt the rules - I have since very much enjoyed passing on this knowledge to others - but I certainly played a few games at school.

I guess I played the occasional game of chess at home with family members or whoever was to hand, until my last year at school, when a friend and I began to play each other. I certainly hadn't ever taken the game very seriously whilst he, on the other hand, had begun to attend the school's chess club. To begin with, at least we were reasonably well matched.

Over time he improved. He bought chess books, studied famous games, strategies, end game theory and opening moves. I didn't. The first piece of chess nomenclature I recall him using was the 'Róy (or Ruy) Lopez opening' (e4 e5/Nf3 Nc6/Bb5) perhaps the most popular chess opening there is.

Fray Rodrigo Lopez de Segura was a Catholic bishop, who in the sixteenth century published the *Book of the Liberal Invention and Art of the Game of Chess* in the attractive town of Alcalá de Henares, birth place of Cervantes and close to Salamanca University, a seat of learning since 1094.

Fray Rodrigo's book was not the first European book on (the modern version of) chess, that honour goes to a Portuguese apothecary called Pedro Damiano, who's *Questo libro e da imparare giocare a scachi et de li partiti* (which roughly translates as *Use this book to learn how to play chess*) was published in Rome in 1521. Fifty years later Fray Rodrigo saw a copy of Damiano's book in Rome and decided he could improve on its various errors. Damiano, for instance, incorrectly suggested that chess had been invented by the Persian king, Xerxes the Great, famous for invading Greece in 480 BC. This wasn't true but it is probably why chess is still known in Portugal as Xadrez. Chess has then, for centuries, courted the interest of players of differing ability, who, in volume after volume, have set out to critique and improve each other's notions of how best to play the game.

I enjoyed, in the early years of our playing, the sense of being always the underdog and winning one game, in say, five. If I won, drew, or even if we'd simply had a particularly close game, my friend and I would often talk afterwards about the 'in and outs' of the game's various stages, the minor battles fought, the major errors made and so on. Eventually, this friend (who incidentally has remained my best friend for over thirty years) got much, much better.

I loved those early matches and it was a shame to see his interest gradually wane as improvements to his game meant our encounters became a foregone conclusion. He would win more and more easily and I would take longer and longer over my moves.

For quite a time the introduction of the chess clock, with its two adjacent clock faces and buttons to stop one's own clock, whilst (re)starting your opponents, could put each player under differing time pressure and allowed our long and drawn out competition to continue. Speed chess was fun, there was less constipated anxiety and indecision on my part, and it allowed for the introduction of time handicaps (he might have only fifteen minutes to play all his moves whilst I had, for example, an hour and so on). Which brought back more of a level playing field even if it was artificial.

However, he started to play more frequently at various chess clubs and further and further afield, with players of increasing quality. He really grew to love the game, its history, the great players, their famous games and their foibles; Bobby Fischer being one of the oddest, saddest and most intriguing. Inevitably as he became more enthused (and a little obsessive) my own drive and incentive to play, no longer having an engaged partner to play with, ebbed gently away.

To the outsider, chess can appear a tedious affair. All that waiting for the other player to move, the silence, the studious, intense and concentrated gazing at the complex of pieces on those sixty-four black and white squares. To those involved, there are many intangible, almost inexpressible, sensations going on behind the fixed stares.

There is something magical about being able to hold a series of 'maybe's' in one's mind and 'seeing' a number of moves ahead. No other game is really quite as mentally taxing (except perhaps Go). I could never go much beyond three, four or perhaps (at a stretch) five moves ahead, after that it required too much brain power to sustain any worthwhile thought. Also, whilst Grand Masters are able to see perhaps thirty moves ahead or play many games simultaneously (against more ordinary mortals), generally they are playing the strongest tactical move with good potentiality. This is wise of course because the total number of actual moves that *could* be made is near infinite - though many of these would be dismissed out of hand as poor moves. To get an idea of the exponential complexity of the moves one could make, at any particular point in a match, I think it's useful to think of or compare the situation, to the parable of Sessa.

Sessa, an Indian minister, who it is said has invented the game of chaturanga (a proto version of chess), is asked by his ruler what he would like as a reward. Sessa says

'Start with one grain of wheat on the first square of the board and double it on every successive square and give me the accumulated wheat as a reward.'

The ruler laughingly grants the request, intuitively feeling that the total will not come to a great amount. If however, you do this doubling each time and assuming there are sixty-four squares on the board, the total number of wheat grains the ruler would have had to give to Sessa comes to an incredible 18, 446, 744, 073, 709, 551, 615.

Similarly, if you think of a chess board with its eight by eight expanse and (to begin with a least) thirty-two pieces, only half of which you can definitely predict the movement of, and all of which, even the pawns, often have multiple potential moves, but also all of which act in concert and combination with every other piece on the board, with the dynamic complex altered every time a move is made, then you begin to get an inkling of how much one has to try and hold in one's head when trying to think ahead in a game of chess.

I have never thought chess boring: tough, tiring, daunting, challenging, difficult, exhausting, frustrating, exasperating and overwhelming maybe but *not* boring. It is a great game BUT if you play often enough, at some point, you will reach a brick wall. You will realize, to improve, you will have to use more than just your native intelligence. You will realize that there are other players that long ago surpassed your very best and sometimes they did that in their junior years.

At that point, you either have to grit your teeth and plough a tremendous amount of energy into improving your game, in only tiny increments, with increasingly diminishing returns or you accept you were not born to greatness, nor can it be thrust upon you! You

withdraw, vanquished, pretty much what I did -
I can't remember the last time I played - or you
find people to compete with who are at your
level. Spending the rest of your life,
appreciating the brilliance of the best in the
world but as an interested spectator and
nothing more.

Chess is certainly a humbling game. A single
move, usually one's own, can undo everything
that went before: the enthusiastic beginning, the
especially good, clever, inspired moves, the
carefully crafted structure and impetus of the
game. All this can be swept away in a second.
One rash 'accident', the unforced error, the
blunder that dawns the moment the piece has
left your grasp and yet failed to announce itself
in the ten minutes of contemplation before
that. This moment of minor tragedy is only one
of the many facets that I love about chess.

Naturally, one's opponent has to see the gaff
one has just made and it is nothing less than a
joyous thrill when they don't. But they rarely do
miss it and their pious smugness in victory can
be almost insufferable. A gracious Zen-like

state is what we wish to possess in defeat, gritted teeth and a weak handshake is commoner.

At either end of the scale, both in the beginner and for the Grand Master, arrogance and pride, whether one likes it or not, are often one's downfall. This is what makes it a great game because whilst it is, in a host of ways utterly meaningless, it does test the emotional mettle one is made of, it is an excellent barometer of wisdom in the storms of intelligence.

Even the best players in the world now, are beaten by computers, so perhaps chess, strictly speaking, does has its limits. There are *only* sixty-four squares after all. But for us humans its capacity, to be different every time we play, is still, more or less, limitless. That fact, will always keep it fresh, even to the most professional player, let alone the humble amateur.

Lisboa

Two Diary Entries

March 2009

Lisbon, that is, *Lisboa*. An unknown city.

My head is hollow from a trans-oceanic flight. I stumble out of the airport, craggy eyed, into bright, blank, mid-day sun. I have only half-slept but the warmth of the sun, on my heavy black jeans and backpack, inspires new energy. I know the Iberian Peninsula well but this is my first time in the capital and I can feel a renewed undertow of excitement in my body.

The bus into Lisbon is simple and direct. In the outskirts, we pass long stretches of, rather grand, old houses, set back from the road. Some neat, with bright, fresh looking, painted exteriors, well kempt gardens. Others, the majority, peeling and cracked, like dusty boxes that have lived out in the sun too long.

The only other landmark, I note, is a

moderately elaborate bullring. It's built with smooth red bricks and towers that remind me of the Kremlin. On second thoughts, it more exactly evokes the semi-circular Exposición building (of 1929) in Seville - which, briefly, appears in David Lean's epic *Lawrence of Arabia* and even more briefly in one of the *Star Wars* prequels. This is in the Maria Luisa Park and adds a certain faded grandeur to that already wonderful spot. Equally, one would say, the bullring adds a certain dangerous magnificence to these otherwise simple suburban surroundings.

Then, seemingly without having taken a turn, we rapidly arrive in Lisboa's central Praça, Dom Pedro IV. I get off the bus and happily put my backpack on the nearest bench. Just as I light a cigarette, a tanned, middle aged man, with a bushy moustache, comes up to me and offers me some hash or *'Chocolaté'* as he calls it. I turn him down with a smile, thinking, if he's an undercover cop that would make a fine start to my trip, being carted off to the local police station.

Looking around, I see, under a clear blue sky, that the praça is spacious and glowing white, with the light of the sun. There are two large circular fountains placed at either end of the praça and a tall column in the centre with a statue of Dom Pedro on top. At one end, off to my left, is a large white neo-classical building with pillars and an architrave but I don't stop to look around. I'm eager to get my room, off load my stuff and change. I find my hospedia, the Bons Dias, quickly, just of the praça behind the railway station. It is, just as I planned, nicely central.

The woman at Bons Dias is friendly and the room fine (though there's not much of a view) but in a matter of minutes I'm back in the Praça which, I soon learn, is actually usually called Rossio by the Lisboan's. No longer physically weighted down I feel pretty light-hearted as I head down the appropriately named Rua Aúrea. I can see, what I think of as the sea, down the end of this gently sloping boulevard and am eager to get to it. That doesn't stop me briefly popping into a very clean and bright bookshop; with its marble floors and cool interior, it's tempting to stay to look around but perhaps later. At the end of Aúrea is what I already know from looking at my map is the Praça Do Comércio. Usually, this would, I think, be a wide open square, today, however, there are builders' boards all around the centre, set too high to see the statue in the middle (without standing on a bollard) and reducing the intended effect of a capital's grandness. Partly due to this, it takes me a moment or two to notice tourists taking photos and turning around I see what they're taking snap shots of, it's a very large triumphal arch, the Arco Da Victoria, through which you can see the Rua Augusta and all the way back up its length, Praça Rossio. Moving down to the waterfront, where there is a gentle bank of steps, leading directly into the water, with two modest pillars either side, I begin to understand (despite the builders' hoardings) the city planners vision. If the visitor comes into Lisbon by boat, up the estuary from the Atlantic, they are greeted by an impressive architectural magnificence, which would refresh any weary traveler, a vista that, through the Arco Da Victoria, takes the eye right into the heart of Lisbon.

Drawn to this vast body of water I put my hand into the gentle waves of the Tagus which has come all the way from Toledo and beyond. Up river, out to the north-east, is the impressive, Golden Gate-like, *Ponte 25th de Abril*. Originally this was the Salazar Bridge, glorifying the Portuguese dictator, but it was renamed, after the date of the Carnation Revolution, which saw the fall of, the equally unpleasant, Estado Novo, in 1974. At least, this is what the young Spanish history student told me later, as we looked over the city, with the aid of the camera obscura housed in one of the towers of the Castelo de São Jorge. I only had a vague idea what a camera obscura was before now but having 'floated over' Lisbon panoramically using one, I think I'm unlikely in the future to forget what they are, nor what a delight they can be.

Next, I looked in at the Marinho da Arcada café, situated on the corner of the Do Comércio, which I recalled as having a connection with Fernando Pessoa. I didn't go in, however, as the customers outside were all talking loudly over lunch and it also looked a bit pricey for my pocket. But wandering away from the café, a few minutes later, I hit upon the Sé, which I thought was the name of the city's cathedral at first but am now pretty sure means 'cathedral' itself.

[Note: Actually 'Sé' is Portuguese for 'See', as in the jurisdiction of a church or an (arch)diocese. The cathedral is often called by the locals simply by the abbreviation 'Sé' or 'Sé de Lisboa' but it is also officially referred to as the 'Sé Catedral de Lisboa' or '(Igreja de) Santa Maria Maior de Lisboa'. 'Sé Catedral de Lisboa' is usually translated into English as the 'Patriarchal Cathedral of Saint Mary the Great'. Hence you can see why I was confused!]

Red and yellow trams run by the cathedral and, this was the first time, I really took in quite how lovely and ubiquitous they are. Though they are a famous sight in the city, they were originally, undoubtedly, a very utilitarian addition. Lisbon is built on seven hills, like Rome, and getting across town on foot must have been a rather sweaty affair before their advent.

My first impression of the Sé was that it seemed rather small. Later I came to appreciate this modesty and see it as part of Lisbon's charm because whilst it has its grand architectural piles, in general, I think of it as a gentle and subtle capital. I ducked in quickly but was tired still and thought I'd look it over on another day. Sat outside, on its steps, for a while but it was hot and I was soon up and away to a little museum close by. This was the Museo Do Teatro Romano, which as its name implies was on the site of an old Roman Theatre but the museum itself seemed to have very few artifacts so I didn't stay long. I was alone in the museum and I only just cottoned on as I left, having been, closely, followed round by an attendant, that they were just closing for lunch.

March 2009

At this moment I'm the only person in the world looking at *The Temptations of St Anthony* by Bosch.

I was head-achy this morning, kept on going back to sleep to try to shake it off. But this is worth it. I had a small coffee in a ratty little place, just up the hill, behind the station. Like injecting new blood in yesterday's corpse; like raising the dead. And so, here I am, alone with a three paneled masterwork. Hieronymus, you feel, knew what a bad night's sleep was, even with, now fresh, morning-eyes, I recognize a certain kind of hell when I see it. Faith too is all around this picture.

Before I got here, after my coffee, I'd waited half an hour or so outside the ruins of a church. Lisbon too has its signs of faith all around. Within the ruin is an archeological museum which I have yet to see. I asked a military guard, from the government building next door, if I was standing at the right entrance. Fortunately, he was friendly, with epaulets and sword he was very neatly but very officiously turned out. Unfortunately, though friendly, he couldn't tell me why the gates of the church weren't open. In the end, all that meant was that I'm now here, in front of *St Anthony,* earlier than I expected.

My first observation of the painting is a simple
one. I prefer it when the flaps of a triptych,
such as this is, are not flat against a wall, as is
the case here. The angled flaps draw you into
the picture just that little bit more. Standing
here alone, I just relish the moment, the luck,
the sheer fortuitousness of me being *here*. How
many eyes, hearts, mouths, have moved before
this picture? How many words have been spilt
around its canvas, trying to capture something
of what it is? And here I am, *the only person in the
world in front it right now*, it's all mine. How lucky
I am.

I break this spell by beginning purposely,
mechanically if you like, to note down some of
the most obvious elements of the painting
before me, this is, I know, a kind of 'warm up'.
So, items: a river runs across the bottom of the
picture, through all three panels, it anchors the
picture. There is a windmill, a Dutch windmill,
in the third panel. So if I didn't already know, I
would've soon guessed this vision was created
by an artist of the low-countries. In the centre
is a broken down place of worship, a tower or
part of a long gone church. On the wall of this

'tower' or 'church' is a depiction of Moses, receiving the word, with in the background, I think, the golden calf. Closer to the canvas now, there seem to be pentimenti, in the water, under the gray platform or jetty, that is in front of the tower. Inside the 'tower' or 'church' is a priest. He is looking directly at us, his head twisted away from the statue of a crucified Christ before which he is kneeling.

At this point, I know, I'm going to spend quite a while in front of this picture, so I take a seat and get out my notebook. I look at Anthony in the third panel; he's now sitting, on the near side of the river, with the Good Book open in his hands. I glance back across to the first panel, in this one he's being carried by three other figures across a short wooden bridge. In the second panel, he's kneeling, making an offering, holding out a bowl of liquid. Observing the three Anthony's makes me more conscious that I need to read the triptych, from left to right. Which, incidentally, reminds me of a time years ago, in the National Gallery in London, when I first realized a similar thing of a Rubens' painting. The Rubens was a single canvas but with its running, half naked, figures repeated across the painting. It was then that I realized, for the first time in my life, that occasionally it was the convention that a painting could be constructed so as to be read like a strip cartoon. This was one of those small observations that incrementally make one realize that you don't just look at paintings but, in fact, you 'read' them. Understanding the conventions, context, and history are primary tools in the language of Art

Bosch's signature is black and gothic. I like it. It is bold, naive, strident. Similarly, I'm gently amused by three teenage girls, who boldly enter the room, naively shuffle about a bit and after a few brief moments stride off, as if all interest in the room has been consumed or evaporated. I guess they're put off by my concentrated note taking (though put off *what* exactly I'm not quite sure).

A fresh glance up at the picture, reveals that behind the central tower to the left, is a burning town, and in the air of all three panels, are various combative engagements and goings on.

Also, there are flying fish ridden by humans and in the river below, boats and boat-birds. The whole picture is quite 'fishy' but also full of eggs and birds and even a large strawberry. The picture is dark but also airy and full of all kinds of unexpected things. Momentarily, I'm reminded of overlooking the city this morning. When having given up on the archeological Museum (within the church) opening, I had wandered behind the ruins and realized that this was where the Santa Justa street elevator emptied out. If you walk over to the elevator, it's rather like approaching a seaside pier but one that floats in the air. From its grill platform and ironwork surrounds you can observe the city beneath and especially onto Rossio. There are no giant fish flying past but down below are the gently wafting streams of the populace going about their multifarious business.

Whatever St Anthony's 'temptation' was *[Note: In brief, it was actually a variety of temptations in the Egyptian desert: two demons in the form of a satyr and a centaur who try to lead him astray, plates of silver and gold coins and a variety of demons and beasts in a cave]*, it is not as dramatic or as major, I think, as

Kazantzaksis's portrayal of Christ's 'Last Temptation'. A temptation that is, which consists of a vision of living another, completely different, life entirely. No, Anthony's temptation is definitely of greater modesty, whilst remaining serious, his request for redemption is more immediate. No doubt, the intention of Bosch being to echo Christ's story, not embody it.

In the central panel, he's beside a lady dressed in finery but with a tell-tale tail. Close by is a small table, which looks like a dice table to me but that is, in all likelihood, more my fancy than reality. Other ladies and several snouty men are close by. When you say 'snouty' with a Bosch picture you mean large boar like snouts, not just men with large noses. So, all are suspect, all fallible, but not quite demons?

Perhaps his temptation is of the carnal sort *[It seems this might have been an embellishment of Bosch's]*? In the third panel, Anthony looks away from the river, towards the opposite bank, on which there is a naked woman, possibly Eve, inside a tree (or *the* tree of Knowledge?). She is draped in red cloth and has a hand, perhaps her own, held over her genitals. Behind her, in the background, is another town in trouble, only this time one that is being besieged, an army held back at its gates. Held back but for how long?

Bosch's depiction of matters is not quite Hell (though there are deformed half-human, half-animal figures etc. and the 'etc.' is hellishly varied) but one might imagine Anthony is passing by an outer ring of Satan's realm?

Whilst Lisboa was warm this morning, as I walked up here to the Museo de Antigua Arte (where *The Temptation* is housed), it certainly was not anything approaching Hell, in fact, it was more like Heaven. At least one of the Praças I passed, Praça de Dom Luiz, with its monument of the Marquis de Sa Da Bandeira and all its trees in blossom, was utterly beguiling, beautiful and just plain gorgeous. I only know the name of the Praça because on my way back, in a cavernous mall on Rua Das Chagas, off the Praça, I bought *What The Tourist Should See* by Fernando Pessoa. Don't get me wrong, the

Praça is small and there's not much to it, so you may not experience my extraterrestrial sensation, but I was in a hopeful, traveler's, energized mood, looking forward to the gallery and enjoying, like never before, the bright sunshine and fresh airs of Lisboa.

There are a dozen or so religious figures draped, in expensive red (ermine?) cloaks, not quite as numerous as the pink blossom but still in excess, Bosch wanting, I presume, to signal the corruption of the church. Some of the animals depicted are partially religiously garbed too, one fish has a bishop's hat, another a church steeple on its back, some carry holy papers or writs. A 'mouse' carries mother and child; in addition, there are three or four nuns in black habits with white trim. One of the nuns is locked inside a 'creature-boat' which has a stingray or skeletal fish for its emblem on a standard. Out of kilter with all this is a single individual with what looks distinctly like a top hat.

Another presence is music, a debauched and corrupting component, filling the fetid air; one can see bagpipe, lyre, trumpet and imagine the weird cacophony underscoring the activity of the inhabitants of this picture. Knives and swords are scattered across the canvas too, punctuating the menace and danger of this world. There is nakedness, cut with blades that stick out from stomach, head and fish. Three Magi types approach the 'dice' table of the central panel. They offer up a tray, upon which a small figurine holds aloft an egg. There are several courtly women and even a couple who could be Mary and Joseph, the patriarch holds out a cup of wine to one of the Magi. But nothing is quite right here. One Magi has an owl on his head (this, I think, a symbol of death) another has a deformed leg and crutch and so on.

On the back (or outer side) of the triptych, the first and third panels have, less complex, grisaille pictures: The first, is Christ on Calvary, with a spot of red, on a staff, held aloft. On the third, a similar scene, but with a rocky hill and a cup and in the lower reaches, holy men, trying to get a couple of criminals to confess or repent their sins before they are crucified.

Eventually, I tired of the Bosch but by then had worked up a thirst for other pictures. In the same room was a Lucas Cranach, a working of the Salomé story (1510), she with furs, St John's severed bodkin offered up on a platter. It's all very clean, clear lines, even the Baptist's bloody neck is neat, Salome herself, has a strikingly modern look (think, Minnie Driver, in period costume).

On another wall, to the left of the Bosch, is the 1521 painting of St Jerome by Albrecht Durer. In my notebook, I copy the initials with which he's signed the picture (a square Germanic type 'A' with a little 'D' between its legs). Behind Jerome, on a rich green background, there is, with 'INRI' printed on it, a wooden, crucified Christ, hanging on the wall. Jerome seated at his desk has one hand to the side of his head. He is wearing a blue/grey hat and robes of red. He has a long, shaggy, white beard. With his other hand, he points a forefinger at, the common reminder of our mortality, a human skull (actually he is touching it). To the left of the skull are an inkpot and quill. On a flat, wooden, reading lectern, before him, is an open book with handwritten text and geometric figures that could be drawings of planets. Below this are another two books, one with a bookmark, on which Durer has painted his initials.

Jerome is old; stern; has thought much, and definitely means it when he says, *'Think on Death, I have, and other deeper things besides!'* When I look at Jerome I'm reminded of other depictions I've seen of him. He is always aged and serious, this is definitely a depiction of a Church Father. You're not supposed to mess theologically with these boys 'cause they know their stuff. Actually, in the next room, I encounter another stern 'Jerome' circa 1525-1550. Anonymous this time but very similar compositionally, there is the desk, book, skull again: with the addition of glasses, what looks like handcuffs(!) and a rotten apple in his hand. He is also bald this time, looking not at the viewer, but up and away. I see later, there's yet another 'Jerome' this time by Jan Sanders van Hemessen (1531). All the same features but set in the desert. Jerome is now a composition well embedded in my consciousness! I reckon I should look him up, and later on, I do, amusingly, I'm informed that he's usually depicted with a lion, the one feature conspicuously absent from the pictures I've just seen.

The skull has made me think of Holbein's *Ambassadors* and oddly enough in the far corner of the room is a (Hans) Holbein The Elder. It's a 1519 'Virgin and Child' but it's very stately and geometric in its layout. V and C are in the centre foreground but all about them are finely dressed ladies of the court, who distract one from the central pairing. In the background is a triumphal arch, part of a series of Roman arches which make up a piece of classical architectural frippery. The capitals of the pillars are decorative Corinthian pieces, made even grander by being off-set with three sets of angels, left, right and centre, each with organ, bible and lute, respectively. Scattered about are many, what I take to be, (generally female) saints. They have dishes, mirrors, swords and flowers. One, as he kicks Satan out of heaven, has his staff stuck through a devil á la St Michael. Another is surrounded by rabbits, rather like St Francis of Assisi.

Further on into the gallery, I see, and largely ignore, as usual, José de Ribera and Zubarán (big, dark and dull canvases on religious subjects). There are, like these two, some classic Spanish painters who I find just *too* gloomy. Other painters are gloomy too, of course, there's a Bruegel the Younger here, his *Works of Mercy* (1564/5), which is not exactly cheerful: the hungry being fed and clothed (it reminds me of a gin swilling Hogarth crowd). Somehow though, Bruegel makes this enlivening and captures one's interest, in a way Zubarán and Ribera never do. The inner aims of a painter are always as important as their manner, style and technique, which can easily drown out the spiritual or intellectual ambition or 'voice'.

Wandering happily along, of a sudden, I come across a huge tapestry. This is not great art but it is phenomenal, grand, striking. It was made in the mid-16th century so its colour is much faded but there's still a strong impact made with an almost cartoon depiction of *The Combat of Hercules*. Hercules looks, appropriately, more Roman than Greek, with a very big nose and battle dress reminiscent of a centurion. With his bow and arrows, he is killing centaurs and rather relishing and reveling in his destructiveness, he is smiling at his handiwork.

This gallery is full of a host of different pictures. Next, I see a Poussin (1594-1665). Actually, it may be a copy or workshop version of his, *Philistines Attacked by the Plague at Ashdod*. I haven't seen many of his pictures and for me, there is an allure attached to him, a mystique, which is I know artificial and a little silly.

In one of his pictures, *Et in Arcadia Ego* (1655), four men point to markings on a tomb and this image is one of the images mixed up in the whole *Holy Blood, Holy Grail* and *Da Vinci Code* concoction. Having been highlighted, for me, in this mass media, popular culture manner, I look at the *Philistines* painting with some interest.

The people in Roman garb are dead and dying in the street, certain figures are foregrounded by a certain perspective and fresh, energetic lighting which is similar to some of Magritte's work and is appealing, in contrast, to the heavier religious paintings in the gallery. I don't spend too long in front of it as I'm tiring. But, I note, that Poussin is a painter I'm waiting to *see clearly,* on another day, when I'm less fatigued and in the right mood and right gallery.

The next oddment is a 7th Century Bodhisattva, a Japanese or Korean, bronze sculpture. Momentarily I soak in its calmness. He holds two fingers up to his face and is sereneness itself. Further on, I'm moving more quickly now, are pots, pans and ceramics which I regard with distaste, thinking, *'This just doesn't interest me in the slightest!'* I am quite the philistine when it comes to objects that are closer to craft than art.

Next, I spot two very large and crude paintings, mechanical, prosaic, practical, both are similar to one another and obviously connected in some way. One is of Dom Alfonso de Albuquerque, who, it turns out, was the First Governor of India (for Portugal naturally). His fellow sixteenth-century companion is Dom Francisco de Mascarenhas. This gentleman is also depicted, with marginally better technique, in a full-length portrait, which, if life-size, means both Dom's were very short and stocky.

These are only of historical interest, the kind of thing one finds reproduced in books on the great Portuguese adventurers and explorers. Following on from this pair are a number of wooden screens from China (Macau, 1708) decorated with battles scenes and events that don't mean anything to me: *The Restoration of Montijo*, *Alconchel* and *Villa Nova del Fresno*. The thing is, I do begin to think, *'Why did the Chinese paint these?'*

Then around the corner, the famous Namban Screens come into view. 'Namban' is not their unique name but rather a type of screen. However, these are apparently, *'…the famous Namban Screens of the Antigua Arte'*. My philistine notion, of crafty stuff being a bit naff, immediately slips a little. These four hundred-year-old screens are beautiful. They are tempera on paper, decorated with gold-leaf, silk, lacquer and metal, and date from 1638-9 and 1640-1, (by Kano Domi and Kano Naizen respectively).

Certainly, my interest is still largely historical. I'm fascinated by these illustrations of the arrival of the Portuguese in Japan, in 1543, but it is the artistry and powerful composition that has drawn me to the subject. It seems that 1543 saw the beginnings of a commercial and cultural exchange between these two peoples from far distant parts of the world.

'Namban Jin' meant *'barbarians from the south'* revealing, that the Chinese felt themselves to be very much more sophisticated than these new arrivees who came in their 'black boats' to Nagasaki.

You read the screen's 'story' left to right. Naizen's screen is of arrival and then departure from Goa (it's known to be Goa because of the architecture and because there are elephants in the scene). Domi's screen shows the arrival of the Jesuit missionaries and includes all the wealth of China: silks and exotic animals being especially noticeable. So much for my dislike of 'craft'.

Very incidentally, I pass a stone-fountain that, Janus-like, has a carving of D. Manuel on one side and D. Leonor on the other (1501-1515). It's here that I appreciate the fact that 'Manueline' is not only a style but refers, in all likelihood, to this Dom Manuel.

I was near dead on my feet by this time. I had gone on looking at more and more of the collection and rather surprised myself at how long I'd kept going. I had just 'had a ball' and realized that, yes, it is necessary to look at one painting carefully but once you've put yourself in the right head space you can quite naturally find a second and even a third wind. However, I felt so exhausted by now that, when I stopped at the six panels of *St Vincent* by Nuno Gonçalves (circa 1465), I was quite possibly *most* pleased that it had, in front of it, a comfortable, padded bench! Without knowing it, I had just parked my bum in front of the prize possession of the Museum and what I now think of as one of the masterpieces of the world.

The six panels are, as the guides say, unusual as they are a collective portrait of fifty-eight people. St Vincent himself is actually on each of the two central panels and so is featured in the collective twice. José de Figueroa (in 1909) called these large religious paintings (originally part of the *retable* in Lisbon Cathedral) *'The panels of friars, fishermen, Infante, Archbishop, knights and relics'* which gives you some idea of the makeup of the participants. Though originally in a cathedral, here now, they seem very perfectly alive.

This set of panels is considered by the Portuguese themselves a masterpiece and they are rightly proud of them. Whilst they don't have the crystal, ice-cool clarity of Van de Weyden, for instance, collectively they are impressive and it's easy to see why they're considered a 'national treasure'. They are full bodied and meaty but not crude; a social, historical and artistic monument.

The many faces are all held quite still. They are passive with far away or rather mid-distant looks and this is, without doubt, very much by design. They are all, every one, held in their own thoughts, not ecstatic or glowing but a group of individuals, *together*. All are soulful, *and* alone, under the eyes of their maker. And, whilst the picture (for one soon thinks of it as *one* picture) is hierarchically arranged, the 'important ones' foreground and centre, with rows and friezes of heads behind. Nonetheless, all seem equal before St Vincent. They are, it is said, venerating the saint but he, like the rest, seems to me to be 'elsewhere' and enveloped in his own thoughts

It's an unusual painting, in style, content and sensibility, especially for this period in Europe. Whilst the painting has *'enormous symbolic importance in Portuguese culture'* quite what the symbolic importance is, is rather ambiguous and has spawned a great many interpretations. One of the many is the notion that Saint Vincent, the patron saint of the capital itself and thus symbolic heart of the new Portugal, was inspiring and patronizing the military expansion into the Maghreb of North Africa. Indeed, I learnt later that Alfonso V, who is kneeling before the saint, was nicknamed, 'The African'. Henry the Navigator and (the future) King John II (here just a boy) are also included for good measure; as is the Infante of Alfonso. One should add, what a passing guide declared, as he described(the picture to his English speaking visitor) that although he was calling these particular personages, 'Alfonso V' and the Infante, 'Elisabeth', no authority could state categorically that it was them.

What's certain, is that the guide calls the faces, resolute, evocative and contemplative, which undoubtedly they are. The picture is both votive and evocative but it also struck me in a very personal way. What I mean to say is, I didn't feel this was just a public piece of art. Nuno has taken a chance, he has grasped the opportunity in this large, probably commissioned piece, to express his *own* feeling; to depict *his* face, his personae, through others. Even the double figuration of Saint Vincent seems to hint at this deeper meaning. How Portuguese this seems to me, in my ignorant, flight-of-fancy-romantic-Portuguese-dreamlike-belief. This, after all, is the land of Pessoa!

It is a beautifully calm picture and, as I say, it also seems one - this six paneled, fifty-eight person, double sainted, plurality - of singular identity and emotion. The faces are described as *'lisa, las caras callado'* (*'flat and silent faces'*). Close-to, the detail on the panels is very fine indeed: it is soft gloved, heavy and light chains, mix with sword and armor, soft doublets and silk raiment's, set off elegant noses, except, strikingly, the nose of the Infante, which is definitely flat and a bit crook. It's all bead and ermine, net and ruffled robe and amusingly, there's a long haired and bearded friar, who looks remarkably like Neil (Nigel Planer) from the TV series *The Young Ones*! This errant infiltration from 20th century British culture seems a disrespectful or jarring thought at first but, after a second or two, I realize it speaks for the picture's *veracity to life* and the constancy of human physiognomy.

It's definitely a game one could play *'spot who looks like whom'* in the painting and in a way that notion spills into the chameleon-like word-play and identity-play of Pessoa, who is floating through my imagination again. He, with his Hetronymic masks, veils and silhouettes of identity; all set amongst a city with Alfama alleys and terrific windways.

At this point, having been scribbling for some hours, with aching hand and sore fingers, I was eager to put my pen away. However, in the next room I was, yet again, inspired to get my notebook out, surrounded, as I was, by a lively and varied collection of 16th century, Portuguese religious paintings: the *Martyrdom of Catherine*, who's being beheaded, surrounded by weird looking figures, irises up in their sockets, so all you can see is the whites of their eyes; a mottled, textured wood panel, depicting a Calvary scene; the magi, like three amazed arrivals, in fancy doublet and jazzy hose.

Among this Portuguese stuff is another Poussin, which, not having seen many or perhaps any of his pictures before, except in reproduction, I'm fascinated to see in the flesh. His name was highlighted for me years ago, as I say, because of *Et in Arcadia Ego* being so often reproduced in the slew of books on the anti-orthodox Christian conspiracy theories about what happened to Mary and the Holy Grail after Christ's death.

The quality of the light in the Poussin is immediate and memorable. He has a strange, gentle texture to his brush stroke which I've not seen before. Depicted, is a gaggle of devotees, about John the Baptist as he preaches. He is cuddling the Lamb of God whilst Christ is being circumcised! The bishop, who's doing the circumcision has, I always find this odd in older pictures, a pair of glasses on, to aid his blade. Lively, lively faces, animated and weird.

An exhausted but elated traveller, I walk out into the garden of the museum, as the gentle, evening sun, drops slowly over the horizon.

Industrial Valentine

One February, when I was a teenager, I hastily posted a Valentine's card through the letterbox of a girl I had a crush on. I was too shy to ever follow this up with anything other than a distant smile and remained an admirer from afar. For a season or two the girl created, within me, intense but confused, clouds of emotion. She made the clouds dark, drew blushes to my cheeks, though just occasionally, it felt like she was a ray of sunshine through that storm of the 'teen-age'.

I mention this puppy-love to demonstrate I have been and can be romantic *and* I am not above such things. However, I have absolutely no doubt that the card I delivered, with racing heart and which declared my *'XXX Love XXX'*, was industrially produced somewhere, by-the-hundreds, if not the thousands. It was not unique or handmade, was certainly not signed, and possibly had no inscription whatsoever.

This year I did not send a card.

Has romance died in my heart? Has age hardened the emotions, as well as the arteries, of the heart? Well, technically speaking, isn't Valentine's for those who *secretly* admire someone but have not professed their feelings as yet? That doesn't wash with my wife. I will give her a card, a small present and a poem. I will, no doubt, make light of the occasion and enjoy the small gift giving and expression of love. I will definitely avoid buying that industrial product, the Valentine's Day Card, and make my own in its stead.

I don't object to such soppy/sweet (or saccharine depending on your viewpoint) expressions of romantic love. Hell, it's better than buying a handgun or voting for a xenophobic politician. What I feel uncomfortable with is the 'industrialization' of such affection.

The tradition of Saint Valentine's Day is, like my emotions all those years ago, a little muddled. To begin with, at least *two* Saints of that name could be celebrated on the 14th

February. The beflowered skull of the first of these, St Valentine of Rome, is exhibited in the 8th century Basilica of Santa Maria. This Valentine or Valentinus (which is from 'valens' the Latin for 'worthy', 'strong' or 'powerful') was martyred in 270 AD. Though even, as early as 496 AD, the details about this Valentine were questioned, by Pope Gelasuis I, who said the events of the saint's life, *were known only to God*.

The Basilica of Santa Maria, incidentally, is much more famous for a, 1st century, sculptured drain cover, *La Bocca della Verità* (or *The Mouth of Truth*) in which many tourists – including Gregory Peck in the film *Roman Holiday* – put their hands. The stone sculpture is a 'lie detector' and it's said if you put your hand in the mouth of Oceanus (the god depicted in its centre), and tell a lie, he will bite it off. When I visited the church and I put my hand in the mouth of god, I told my future wife that I loved her. I still have the hand, so, as far as I know, Oceanus is still a living god.

The second major candidate is Valentine of

Terni, a bishop, martyred, it is usually said, in the reign of Emperor Aurelian (270-75 AD). This Valentine was, as was his running mate above, originally buried somewhere along Rome's Via Flamina, on 14th February, but had his remains moved to the *Basilica di San Valentino* in Terni, Umbria.

The tourist board, in the province, likes to say, Terni is, *'The City of Lovers'* but, like Valentine of Rome, not much is actually known about him. In fact, Jack B. Oruch, an academic at the University of Kansas, wrote that *'Abstracts of the acts of the two saints were in nearly every church and monastery of Europe'.* Clearly, stories and traditions surrounding the two Saints, have had many opportunities to be conflated.

It was Oruch's research, in the nineteen eighties, that suggested it was actually Chaucer, who first associated the saint with Love and thus invented Saint Valentine's Day as we know it. *'Late in the fourteenth century'* Oruch says *'Chaucer and his friends John Gower, Sir John Clanvowe, and the Savoyard soldier-poet Oton de Grandson wrote poems in which St. Valentine figures as a patron of the mating of birds and human lovers'.*

However, it is specifically Chaucer's poem, *Parlement of Foules* (or *The Parliament of Birds)*, written to celebrate the anniversary of the engagement of Richard II to Anne of Bohemia, which Oruch focuses on.

The narrator in the poem, begins by reading Tully (Cicero), goes into a dreamlike state, in which he passes through a beautiful landscape and then encounters the Queen of Nature, who is overseer to a 'parliament of birds', who debate, on who will be their mate. The parliament is held on Valentine's Day, when, as Chaucer says, *'every bird cometh there to choose his mate'.* The birds debate while three tercel (male) eagles try to win the hand (as it were), of a formel (female) eagle. The tercel love-birds, actually fail in the suit, and are told to wait another year but the connection, with Saint Valentine and Love, had been made.

Valentine's Day, as with much in our culture, has lost its innocence. It has been hijacked by commerce and mass production like most popular celebrations. The truly folkloric, no longer exists, for much of the world. We all know it, and that's why we all, at times, search for or yearn for greater self-expression than the commercial, mass produced item, embodies. We may romanticize the past but we also wish to romanticize the present.

Industrialization, in and of itself, is not an evil. But it does seem to sully, tarnish or take the edge off personal expressions of love, replacing the individual, natural and folksy, for the mass, corporate and generic. Perhaps there is no 'going back' to folk art or 'Nature'. We have transformed our histories and the content of the natural world so dramatically, repackaged our cultures, murdered so many species, altered so many plants etc. that it's impossible to know what that 'return' would mean or entail. Put another way, the 'nature' of human beings is to be creative, destructive and industrious, whether that means making Art, fire or genetically engineered entities of various sorts. We desire and create change.

How we develop and use our industrial processes to underpin culture, how we utilize, exploit and/or replenish nature, and what political system we 'umbrella' all this under... well, that is where the morality comes in. The global capital system we have is obviously a poor system in many ways. How can one *not* call it that when millions of people are starving or living pitiful lives, when, clearly, we have the technical and industrial capacity for that not to be the case?

Capitalism, after all, with its notions of hierarchy and competition, is *designed,* by default, to have such inequalities. Capitalism's rationale is the division of riches, its premise, is that it's good to have winners and losers. Rational, equitable distribution of wealth, is anathema. The notion of truly mutual co-operation, even love, as a basis for human interaction, is within a system of Capital, at best, an occasional epiphenomenon or incidental by-product. Human, cultural and natural resources are, primarily, seen as *there* for exploitation by the extreme minority. *'The poor are always with us' 'the market dictates...'* is the rhetoric of such willful 'failures' to control our destiny or rather act in the interests of others, as well as ourselves. The extremes of wealth, between the citizens of the world, the continual wars and hate between nations, and so on, are seen as inevitable and normal.

Even, as a love-sick teenager, I knew, such tired impressions of reality were only a cardboard approximation of the truth. I knew (or could sense at least), by its poverty of expression and imagination, that the mass produced Valentine's Day card existed, only because some industrialist insisted that his factory should produce it, for profit. The cultural and material pollution of the world with such manufactured images was, and is for money. Love costs more.

Volcano Theatre and Nascent Writing

The piece below was a short review I wrote over fifteen years ago. Rather than 'edit out' it's rather breathless style I decided to leave it, more or less, as it was when it was first published in PAN Magazine (Summer Edition, no.6, 1998). *I think the rawness of the writing captures both my enthusiasm and my naiveté. Volcano have for decades been one of the most innovative and inspiring of theatre companies. They say of themselves and their original impetus,* "Theatre had lost its way. It had missed the energy and impossibility of punk, the obviousness of state socialism, the adrenaline of sport."

There has been and continues to be a rather hidden tradition of incredibly energetic, challenging and dynamic physical theatre companies in Britain who go unnoticed by large parts of the population. I was lucky enough to *work on two shows (*Day Trip to Troy *and* Suit of Lights*) with Pete Sykes of RAT Theatre and so experienced firsthand the dedication and sheer physical brilliance of one of the best of these companies. Other companies such as Frantic Assembly, Hoipolli and DV8 carry on this tradition inspired (and trained) by mildly better known luminaries of the previous generation such as Jerzy Grotowski, Peter Brook, Jacques Leqoc and others.*

The review below talks of the 'Writer's Workshop' week that I attended but in subsequent years I also took both the Actor's and Director's workshops which were equally exceptional and included memorable contributions from the likes of actor and TV presenter Ken Campbell and Artistic Director of the Royal Court Theatre, Max Stafford-Clark. In the modern era it is great that much of the work of these theatre companies is now captured and catalogued digitally for future generations. However, it still remains true that nothing quite replaces the energy in the room of live performance, especially when the essence of that performance is physical.

Revolution: Voices in Opposition

'A festival of poetry and dramatic writing organized by Volcano Theatre Company in association with the Dylan Thomas Centre in Swansea'

-Publicity blurb-

Driving into darkest Swansea, on a blustery Welsh mid-morning, is not necessarily the most exciting of experiences but on my first day of *Revolution'98* I was both excited and rather tense. For the last three or four hours, on the drive down from Milton Keynes, I had been mulling over what I might be greeted with when I got to my final destination.

The Dylan Thomas Centre sits a stone's throw from the small docks and jetties of Swansea Bay. I know this almost only by hearsay because in my week in this bay side town I was only ever to see the small fisherman's boats, holiday cruisers, speed boats and whatnot at a distance, on my short walks from the Centre to *The Queens*.

The Queens being a large, friendly, sometimes raucous, public house of the older sort, with no 'theme' in sight - except perhaps the odd print on the smoke-stained walls of sea craft which, like their owners, had long since passed away. My week was to be so busy with focused, intense conversation and 'fags' down *The Queens* that I went on the attractive beach Swansea has only once and briefly at that. I had bigger fish to fry I guess.

The 'tenseness' I mentioned was the product of my attending, for the first time in my life, a 'Writer's Workshop'. *'Don't ask me!'* I said, to those who'd asked, in the weeks before the trip, *'Haven't a clue what you do at a Writer's Workshop'*. And, standing outside the big wooden doors of the Dylan Thomas Centre that morning, I still didn't.

What did one do at such a thing? How was the muse *made* to sing? With humanity and soft spoken suggestion or by the torture of open trial? Were each of her children (i.e. one's own scraps of newly born text) to be mercilessly torn apart, line by mewling and puking line, to the inner glee of a huddle of other proto-writers? It would be nice to say only the former happened, which I can, as it happens to be true (i.e. soft spoken, humane suggestion). The latter is, however, what I, in my febrile state of mind, imagined might be the case. My stomach wrenched and twisted regularly, as I heard my freshly penned pieces read aloud, to and by, what I have to honestly say were the smiling, appreciative, supportive faces of my fellow authors.

The first day however, I was most confident and with friendly introductions over we had what was to be probably one of the most productive days of the week. Fiona Sampson, a poet [and the first woman to edit the illustrious *Poetry Review* since Muriel Spark], took the session and had us delve into our earliest memories for a multiplicity of different emotional and poetic directions. Lots of short exercises to enliven the mind. I was swept back to childhood memories of toddling about on a beach, in Wales, in red frilly swimming trunks.

Liz Lochhead, Scottish playwright, performer and regular broadcaster for Radio Four, supplied us, on the second day with stacks of very practical approaches to the writing of monologues and dialogues. This advice mostly concerned what she called 'the gap' between the manifest motivations of characters and their true sub-textual drive. She and I locked horns, for quite some time, over my use of the theosophic term 'Akashic records' which she thought much too obscure and esoteric. In the evening she also performed, very effectively, an hour's worth of her poetry and monologues with an observational humour tinged with Celtic irony.

Day three we were confronted with the techniques of non-retinal writing, 'chance' or 'found' writing, assemblage, collage, cut-up and automatic writing. The challenge, of finding and forcing the latent in all the texts around us, was presented by the poet (and one time editor of *Second Aeon*) Peter Finch. Again, as with Liz Lochhead, Finch performed in the evening and discussed his work and methods throughout the day. My abiding memory, however, was of a fellow writer and actor, who produced a very comic piece, simply by replacing many of the nouns in a 'found' text with the word 'Penguin'. It was by far the most amusing and successful penguin of the day and our shared laughter, as he read it out, will stay with me for a long time.

The group, locked in a room all day, writing, debating, revising and performing pieces, went off to a greasy spoon cafe at lunch times, occasionally, talking of things other than writing, but not often. Then, after the evening event, we would simply head off to *The Queens* or a late night drinking den called *Mozart's,* continuing the animated discussions about all forms of writing and performance and hammering out new ideas and inspirations by the hat full. It was fast becoming one of those weeks which make you say, *'This is how life should be all the time!'*

Day four brought a change of pace with Claire Dowie, a London based comedienne and writer of 'Stand Up' Theatre. She has written for Gay Sweatshop Theatre Company, Central Television, BBC Radio and won *Time Out* and

Evening Standard awards for her darker, more serious, play *Adult Child/Dead Child*. This day allowed the professional actors in the group to perform or improvise or expand characters they had been working on. It was very interesting to see a variety of types of actor create roles in this way.

The next day brought into our arena Ed Thomas, probably the best known playwright in Wales at the moment. *[A recent article in* The Independent *quotes a story of his about his inspiration for his play,* Gas Station Angel, *'When Ed Thomas was six years old, he fell into the river near his home in Cwmgiedd, while swinging from a tree trying to impress a schoolmate. By the time he had been fished out, 25 minutes later, his skin had turned blue. He was pronounced dead by his uncle, so efforts were focused on saving his mother, who had waded out into the flood tide even though she couldn't swim. Ed Thomas survived because a man with "fleshy, alcoholic lips" gave him the kiss of life.' This gives a little bit of the flavour of the man.]* He has written and directed eight plays for Fiction Factory, most of which have been translated and performed all over the world. His film *House of America* was shown during the evening slot and with its 'state of the Welsh nation' undercurrent and Greek tragedy structure created a distinct and dark mood that night.

Thomas' workshop was also, for myself at least, the most conceptually challenging and inspirational of the week. He began his session by putting an empty chair in the middle of the room and stating that there was no such thing as character (the complete reverse of Liz Lochhead's approach). We then 'cannibalized' and dismantled one of his own plays and started rewriting it. In truth, he felt that writing workshops were in most senses redundant, the only way to learn to write was to write. That is simple, direct, even blindingly obvious but in his workshop and especially in discussions during breaks, he translated, exuded even, the emotional weight of that 'freedom' dramatically. There were people in the group who found his contradictions and the fallacious nature of some of what he said and professed, at its core, a rather hollow, theatrical display. Having a chat and a smoke in between times, it was this spirit, attitude and iconoclasm and absolute lack of regard for theory that I found most appealing.

Nigel Jenkins, the following day, provided, for some, the antidote to Thomas' deconstructionism. Jenkins is a Welsh poet, journalist and travel writer, who writes just the most beautiful poetry, which he reads well too. He performed a 'surgery' on pieces we had with us and which we'd written before the week began. On this penultimate day, in the gentlest of sessions he created one of the most thoughtful, pleasant and instructive days of the lot.

I haven't mentioned Paul Davies or Fern Smith from Volcano Theatre Company who organized the whole event. They took part in all the workshops and like the impressive group of writers they invited, were extremely friendly, open, encouraging and inspirational. Their ten or so years, as a dynamic and innovative theatre company, was shown by the quality of the writers they attracted to the event and the quality of their own contributions to all aspects of the week.

The week finished with a debate, led by *The*

Guardian theatre critic David Adams, who spoke of the disastrous consequences, for experimental and 'oppositional' theatre in Wales, of the new funding structure brought about by the National Lottery. This talk was an education in itself and was worth the trip to Swansea alone.

I have visited Wales a dozen times since I was a child - and holidayed here in my red, frilly swimming trunks - but this was, as if it were actually, the first time I'd been. I had met and communicated properly, if only briefly, with some of the most interesting and warm hearted of people. Besides the importance of its denizens it was also personally important and symbolic for myself. It was the first time I called myself a writer in front of strangers. They may have made me nervous and tense at times but they never made me doubt that such ordeals are worth it. To any potential writer I would say, *'Go!' Revolution* is a great destination.

A Bolt of Lightning: RAT Theatre

Apart from a symposium, at the University of Aberystwyth in 2007, concentrating on RAT's work in 1972-3 (with special attention to Hunchback, Blindfold *and* 'British Alternative Theatre of the Seventies'*) there is, as far as I know, very little written material available on RAT Theatre.*

The following essay then, is a curio that I have included here because it will, I hope, help preserve a small piece of British theatre history.

When I was nineteen I had the good luck to work with a theatre company called RAT *(originally the acronym stood for* Ritual And Tribal Theatre*) on a summer school project and a piece of theatre called* Day Trip to Troy. *For me, as a youngster, it was a formative and autobiographically speaking, seminal experience.*

The company and especially the principal actor,

Pete Sykes, were inspirational. In the month or so that we worked on creating the play, I learnt, without quite realizing it, an immense amount about the European theatre traditions of Grotowski, the basics of 'physical theatre' and the essence of how brilliant Samuel Beckett's work is, especially, when performed to rigorous standards.

The latter of these (i.e. Beckett's work) I experienced second-hand by watching Sykes and the other actors of RAT, rehearse and perform, Act Without Words part I *&* II *and* Play. *The latter was amazing because of the technical pressure it put the actors under. Four actors are encased in urns for the duration. They speak, rapidly without pause, only when a light is flicked onto their urn. For both the lighting technician and actor this is a tough test of physical and mental endurance. Sykes himself, in* Act Without Words part I, *left an indelible impression that has never left me. Every time he entered onto stage, which must have been thirty times, he did it with a forward somersault, where he landed, squarely and what looked painfully, flat on his back. He would* *airily brush himself off and carry on.*

I have seen other actors perform this play but never with Sykes' intensity, nor with such physical courage. Pete and his fellow actors were utterly committed and serious artists and I have rarely had the privilege of acting with such dedicated souls since.

As is often said, theatre, because it's 'live', is singular and unique every time. That only really matters, however, if the actors are dedicated to giving a unique performance. In most professional theatre productions the play is somewhat mechanically reproduced, sometimes to a very high standard, but as a facsimile of the playwrights' original. By which I mean, the play has been rendered an object, solid, uniform and pretty much, without blemish. This allows audiences to see the same show, more or less, night after night. However, there are performers for whom each performance is closer to a sacred act. It is a repeated ritual, thus a 'facsimile', and yet it is also unique, filled with a moment to moment reality. I won't (can't perhaps) elaborate much, except to say Pete Sykes was truly an awesome actor, an actor for whom acting was sacred. Full of an animalistic power, he had within his movement on stage, the power of a bull in the corrida. Whilst his eyes, face and physiognomy maintained a burning intelligence.

Off stage I found him to have the air of a rebel. He was someone that I, as a young man, admired, aspired to be like and was a bit scared of. I obviously left my own impression on the company, as several months after the project had ended, I got a call, asking if I would like to 'fill in' for one of the actors who had had to drop out of a show due to appendicitis.

It was the best two weeks of my life (up to that point) rehearsing as a professional actor for the first time. The play by Joyce Holliday was called Suit of Lights *in which I, principally, played a bull. I was on a bike with a metal cage over me shaped as the bull's body, with a fibre glass adjustable bull's head at the front. I had to twist, turn and snarl, and learn the complex maneuvers of a bullfight, with Pete as the toreador. The stage was in the round and replicated a bullring with barriers fencing the audience off from the stage area. I wheeled, butted, span and turned so rapidly that I came off-stage with bloody shins. It was exhilarating for me and had the audience pulling back, as I accelerated toward them, turning, just in time, so as not to plunge into them!*

It is a sadness to me now that the work of RAT has largely been forgotten. That's partly why I reproduce the piece below (somewhat altered) which I wrote but which was heavily based on an autobiographical audiotape that Pete Sykes loaned me.

In truth, most of the essay echoes Pete's voice and opinion rather than my own. At the time, I probably wouldn't have known Merce Cunningham from a lamp post, let alone who or what 'New Dance' was or Wilhelm Reich and his theories of biological energy and the Orgone (it was Reich, incidentally, who coined the term 'The Sexual Revolution'*).*

When I visited Pete in Newcastle-under-Lyme, sometime after Suit of Lights, *he was kind enough to put me up for a few nights. I had many a long and inspired and inspiring conversation with him. The detail of those conversations, with Pete, who was a knowledgeable and witty raconteur, I've forgotten. In fact, I had mostly forgotten at the time, due to the fact that they were usually conducted, whilst I attempted to keep up with his rapid and gargantuan consumption of Guinness, down the pub. The next morning it was rather like that line about the sixties, if you could remember them (in my case the events of the previous night) you weren't really there.*

I do, nonetheless, remember his tired resignation and frustration at the funding in England for small scale theatre companies such as RAT. He spoke, longingly, of semi-retiring to Greece (where he was recording his comments) and performing in the open air, in the land that originated Tragedy and where they still appreciated his artistic endeavours.

He is dead now and whether he ever got to Greece I don't know but I like to think of him there, amazing and stunning audiences, until the end.

I imagine his audience, who began as strangers,

walking away from the show in animated,
friendly conversation, talking of what they have
just seen and experienced, as the mellow sunlight
fades on another unique performance and a life
time's dedicated work.

'Actors should be like Martyrs, burnt at the stake,
signaling through the flames.'

-Antonin Artaud-

First heard in 1968, by RAT Theatre Company's founding member and Artistic Director, Peter Sykes, Artaud's definition has become both an inspirational and representative standard which the company attempts to adhere to and obtain.

The first trace of the company's existence and appearance in the wider world, came with a 1970-1 adaptation of Milton's *Paradise Lost.* The company, in genesis at the time, consisted of seven students from Keele University. *Paradise Lost* was performed at *The Sunday Times'* National Student Drama Festival (of 1971) [see however the addendum to Post Script below] and was described in *The Financial Times* as an, *'Incredible sub-Grotowski piece'*.

The company prided itself on the complex rigorous physical training and discipline that all its actors went through (and unknowingly, at least initially, replicating the practice within Jerzy Grotowski's Theatre Laboratorium).

It was not until three shows later however, with the award winning production of *Hunchback* (1972) (coincidentally, the oriental Year of the Rat) that the company solidified and gained its first name, Ritual and Tribal Theatre Company, which suitably reflected their stylistic bias at the time. Critics compared this early work not only with Grotowski but also with Julian Beck and his Living Theatre. Sykes maintained, however, that at this embryonic stage, he and his fellow actors had neither seen, nor heard of either.

The initial direct influences were, it seems, of a broader eclectic and esoteric wash. Literary, terpsichoreal, artistic and cultural references cited by Sykes include, the writings of Wilhelm Reich, such as, *Character Analysis* and *The Function of the Orgasm*. What he calls the 'masterwork' of Mircea Eliade, *Shamanism:*

Archaic Techniques of Ecstasy, the notions of Yin and Yang, Tai Chi and oriental philosophy generally, along with Antonin Artaud's Theatre of Cruelty, summarized in Artaud's book *The Theatre and It's Double.*

Other great influences in the visual arts included, the Expressionism of Edvard Munch, the surrealist paintings of René Magritte and the progenitor of modern sculpture, Auguste Rodin and his work. As for dance, in the late nineteen sixties and early seventies the boom of what was subsequently called 'New Dance' was in full swing, with dancers and choreographers, such as, Martha Graham and Merce Cunningham, breaking exciting new ground.

As part of this outsider zeitgeist, RAT Theatre was born with a methodology that aimed to develop a direct challenge to what they saw as the sterility and paucity of post-war works, such as, Sartre's existentialism and ironically (given my experience) what they perceived, at the time, as the nihilism of Beckett.

RAT were never a mainstream theatre company and since the heyday of their early years have never received a great deal of critical or academic attention. This is a shame, especially when one considers the ephemeral nature of theatre and stage acting.

At present, the company is made up of five members. Pete Sykes is the artistic director, actor and creative driving force behind most projects. Sykes comes up with the seed of an idea which the company then commissions a writer to develop into a play. Although the company is democratic in its work processes with much debate, improvisation and collaboration Sykes is the final arbiter, in relation to artistic decisions and direction. He also makes the long term financing and accounting decisions.

Sykes is aided, in financial matters, by Gill Gill, who is the co-ordinator of day to day administration and bookings. She is a long time actor within the company and has been part of RAT since 1972. Their principal designer and technician is Hilary Hughes, a member since 1973, who occasionally acts in smaller roles. Yvonne Smith, another of the principal actors, and member since 1976, helps with the myriad of additional tasks that any small scale touring company has in abundance. Beth Ashton, the youngest and newest member, is a recent performing arts graduate who worked with the company during her degree and most recently acted for the company in *Ager Sanguinis*.

The structure of the company is flexible, allowing actors to flow in and out of active participation, as the need arises. In its first fifteen years RAT has had around twenty full time artists (excluding quite a number of 'temporary contract' artists).

The co-operative nature of the organisation means none of the roles are mutually exclusive but for practical reasons, at any one time, everyone will have clearly allotted tasks. To an extent this 'non-exclusivity' allows individual interests to flourish. In addition, it has become an intrinsic part of operations, a tradition almost, that every member of the company learn a new skill each year. Recent skills have included fire eating and stilt walking.

The ever evolving nature, of company member's skills, is part of a wider ideology with relation to performance. On stage there are no completely fixed rules, fresh and unique is preferred, over and above, rigid 'perfection'. There is an open relish within the company for tales of how actors, with a limited contract, have been deliberately made to 'corpse' on stage, when the more permanent company members have felt the new actors have fallen back on mechanical acting techniques. Standard practices in professional theatre such as 'marks' on the stage floor, to help actors 'find the light', are eschewed for a more organic sensibility that responds to the new within each performance.

The amount a play develops within performance will vary. If the project is an original script, constructed through company improvisation, naturally this leads to a greater tendency to 'rewrites'. If the project was commissioned, the playwright's script, is less likely to be altered.

Whatever the case, within each play there are, what Sykes terms, 'Sign Posts', which each actor will be aware of and *through* which they will travel but *in-between* which they can instigate a high level of spontaneity. Within the confines of their role (and with a controlled sympathy toward fellow actors) the actor is free to interpret as they see fit. In this way the chemistry of each performance can lead to explosive moments 'improvisation'.

Since its inception a number of other companies have come under the umbrella of RAT Theatre. All of these are still in existence, except Coypu Music Theatre, which co-opted the help of music students from Keele University (and ceased to exist in 1977).

Mouse Theatre is by far the most prolific of these offshoots having a tally of fifteen original shows to its name. The company's creation came about, in 1975, when a member of the audience suggested that whilst RAT could capture the attention of serious and dedicated theatre goers they would not be able to entertain children. Every year since, Mouse Theatre, under the direction of RAT members, has produced a summer and a winter show. Usually for primary school children and usually with didactic and educational aims, on subjects such as dental hygiene, picking up litter and so on. These have proved immensely entertaining and popular with schools.

A second children's company, Squirrel Theatre, largely runs theatre workshops and then devises plays with children as the actors (its name came from a nine year old, who said, *'Doing workshops with you is like storing nuts for winter'*).

Circus Muskrat Theatre is a shop window, for RAT actors, to show off their circus skills. Dormouse Theatre came out of hiding in the early eighties and provides story telling services for public libraries. Lastly, Beavers Theatre, is the provocative (or depending on your perspective, tongue in cheek) name of *'a company run by women for women'* and represents, and is, a response to the feminist movement of the eighties. Beaver Theatre is also the company which has moved furthest away from under the 'umbrella' of RAT and is likely to be seen as an entirely independent entity in the future.

In whatever guise RAT has performed it has maintained a consistent approach to stage design and costume. RAT has never tried to be realistic in its staging rather the set and design elements have always been impressionistic. The different forms one can use, to create impressions or evoke scenarios, are infinitely more interesting and variable, Sykes would argue, than trying to maintain a realism which is often ineffective, even if achieved. In the same way that words are often used minimally or inventively in their shows, so the physical paraphernalia of traditional props, costume and set are kept at a minimum.

In fact, the company has shifted, from its more elaborate early years, to a pared down version of design. For instance, the company would not now use the thousand yards of scaffolding, to enclose its audience (and give them *'a taste of hell'*), as it did with *Paradise Lost* in 1970. After a decade and a half of touring, primacy is given to the practical feasibility of transporting any new set. Partially, Sykes admits, that with exception of Beth, the rest of the company members are over thirty and they simply find the idea of touring with 'difficult' sets less appealing. The notion of 'travelling light' has embedded itself and preservation of energy for performance is seen as more important. Such are the practicalities for many small scale touring companies.

In the early seventies the extreme physical style of production earned the company a controversial reputation. The Arts Council of Great Britain, in 1974, went as far as calling the company *'Aggressive and masochistic'*. The Arts Council subsequently axed the company's grant, following critical arguments, over *Blindfold*, RAT's contribution to the Nuclear Disarmament debate which was raging at the time. *Blindfold* was an adaptation of an H.G.Wells story whose premise was that, *'After a nuclear holocaust it's the lowest, most basic level of humanity which survives.'*

In spite of, and in contrast to, the funding body's reaction, these early years also saw RAT gain both national and international recognition. They were the British representatives at ten European arts festivals, winning major awards at five of these events.

Perhaps the greatest success in the first five years of the company's existence was *Judas*, premiered at the Edinburgh Festival, in 1973, but reworked several times in the following years. The show toured Britain and then played at festivals in Belgrade, Yugoslavia, Italy and had a season at the Mickery Theatre in Amsterdam.

The premise for *Judas,* originated by Sykes, was that Jesus had betrayed Judas and not vice-versa. The idea being that Judas has faithfully believed, that when the Messiah arrived, he would come with '*all guns blazing*', strike down the Bad and return the earth to the Good. The nature and actions of Jesus, a gentle, forgiving preacher, does not fit the bill. Thus his actions are perceived as a betrayal in Judas' eyes.

Sykes initially had a plot synopsis, consisting of eleven points, which was then improvised on, by the company, until the 'points' had expanded to fifty and the script had been distilled and cut, edited and re-edited to its essentials. As Sykes puts it, '*It was like drawing a skin taut over a drum, to perfect the resonance.*'

RAT, in its earlier incarnations, was perhaps always orientated towards a central European theatrical tradition. '*European audiences are much more honest than English ones'* says Sykes with approval, *'...the European audiences show if they are bored and do not politely sit through, as an English audience would.'* In 1977, however, the intensity of this attitude and perhaps the exhaustion of seven years of hard work, led to a temporary hiatus.

After a break, the company was reformed and changed its name, from Ritual and Tribal Theatre Company, to the less 'aggressive' Rodent Arts Trust Theatre Company. Reflecting a (temporary) change of attitude, for their first project after the 'split', the new company co-opted the help of an up and coming playwright, Peter Flannery (most famous now, for his play, then TV series, *Our Friends in the North*).

Flannery's previous play, *The Bodies,* was an adaptation of *Therese Raquin* by Emile Zola and his approach to theatre was traditional, literary and concentrated on 'the word', rather than the physical components that were RAT's strong suit. *Boy's Own Story* (1978), the play he wrote for RAT, had a goalkeeper conduct a monologue, between saves, at a football match.

The physical element was, of course, still present but was much less to the fore. In between great feats of athleticism, Sykes (who played the keeper), would absorb the audience in emotional and romantic images of the sport, building things up to an atmospheric crescendo, then sharply cutting them down with a single statement of utter realism.

In the social environment of the time, with increasing football hooliganism, it aroused strong and sometimes diametrically opposed reactions. As Sykes remembers, *'It was powerful enough to cause the departure of a whole football team midway through a performance in one theatre. Whereas in an upper class ladies club it had them* "rolling in the aisles".'

Whilst this stylistic digression was successful, Sykes, when I interviewed him, was still more interested in talking of projects, such as *Ager Sanguinis*. The Battle of Ager Sanguinis (or The Battle of the Field of Blood) was an encounter, in which a crusader army was defeated by a Muslim army from Aleppo, in the twelfth century. However, it was not the subject matter that Sykes wished to talk about, his primary interest was in conveying the working methodology the company had adopted.

Sykes said of his directorial role on the project, *'I'm not a Machiavellian dictator, nor am I the director who says,* "Oh dahling, that's very nice. Now, do it again but do it better." *No, I see myself more as an orchestral conductor who must coax every minute nuance out of the score.'* The method Sykes applied to the play was, primarily, to approach it with a multi-dimensional, physical training programme for the actors, involving Tai-Chi, bio-Olympics, bio-mechanics, Alexander Technique, voice work, general centering and ground work. His aim? To loosen up the mental and physical 'blocks', completely freeing the sub-conscious mind and releasing physical restraints, to bring about the unification of the mind and body, so the two became one. *'This achieved, it was then necessary for each of the actors to be introduced to the psychological centre of the character they were playing'* explained Sykes, the idea was, *'To discover [their] depths and obtain, in performance of the character, a certain purity.'*

With this base, the play soon changed organically, from its original state (similar to that of *Judas'* structure and 'points') into something almost unrecognizable. One of the biggest differences was that the already sparse dialogue became Latin. The words did not have to be understood in the conventional sense but they were still used to communicate. *[N.B. We used similar techniques on* Day Trip to Troy. *I recall, in particular, singing and speaking in Spanish and a South African tribal tongue, having undergone, in addition, weeks of physical training which included diving off high towers into the arms of fellow actors]*.

RAT has then developed from the youthful company that had, at the heart of its *raison d'etre,* the desire to shock or disarm its self-satisfied, polite English audience. It has, over the years, developed what Sykes would call a more *'mystical'* aim (for both actor and audience). RAT rarely succeeds, in his opinion, with shows where theme and story are conveyed solely or, in the main, by way of a clever script. Such plays lack, what Sykes calls, *'purity'*.

A case in point is the clash of cultures that

occurred when Joyce Holliday, known as a community and regional theatre writer, was commissioned by RAT to write *Suit of Lights* about bullfighting.

Holliday introduced a polemical and political strain of argument, to the script, that Sykes disliked. His main comment, on his interaction with Holliday, was to quote favourably, one audience member's reaction to the play, *'The story was okay but instead of the bullfight being a quarter of the show it should have been the whole of the show. It was breath-taking.'* Perhaps, unsurprisingly, no mention of the play is made in either *The Guardian's* or *The Independent's* obituary of Joyce Holliday (who died in 2002).

Reiterating his own position, Sykes said, *'Human emotions and drives are basic and constant throughout history and are below the surface of all dramatic events, however intellectualized and socially defined they become.'*

The history of RAT theatre is divided into three time periods:

The first period, 1970 to 1975: This was when

the youthful company (kept afloat by funding from The Arts Council of Great Britain) toured Europe and won awards. The plays performed were devised, innovative and in step with the social climate of the era.

The second phase, 1977 to 1984: Under the new banner of the Rodent Arts Trust, the company settled, physically and economically, into the West Midlands Arts Region, by whom they were funded. In this period all of their plays (for adult audiences) were created by commissioned writers or were established works. Whilst the shows were socially relevant they were performed in a 'haze' of recession, politicians and public alike, searching for inspiration and perhaps not finding it in the theatre.

1984 to the present: The mid- (or post-)recession is, as Sykes asserts, the backdrop to the start of the third period in RAT's history. RAT Theatre Company is, at present, taking stock, pausing and recharging. The most probable avenue RAT will take will be to relocate and move, from its present home in

Newcastle-under-Lyme, Staffordshire, to Canon Frome, Herefordshire, where Beaver Theatre is already based.

Whatever their future, Pete Sykes and his company will, no doubt, continue creating challenging theatre. The company have never courted fame and is not a corporate entity, it is, as its members have always wished it to be, 'on the fringe' but *not* of the obscure.

As Antonin Artaud said, *'Theatre should be like a bolt of lightning from a clear blue sky'*. From audience feedback, it can safely be said that frequently, RAT Theatre is, still, that unexpected bolt from the blue.

Post-Script

In the course of revising this essay I came across the book, *Mickery Theatre: An Imperfect Archaeology* by Mike Pearson (one of the academics behind the symposium at the University of Aberystwyth and for a short while [1972-3] a member of RAT itself). Below, is a short excerpt from the book which, I think, gives a sharper edged view (than my youthful prose) of quite how explosive RAT Theatre was in its early years.

Previous, to the passage below, Pearson has just quoted the programme notes of the 1973 World Theatre Festival, in Nancy, which say RAT have taken Grotowski and Artaud *'to their furthest extremes'*. He also mentions Peter Brook and Charles Marowitz's 'Theatre of Cruelty' season, with the RSC, in 1964, as context for what was happening at the time. However, RAT Theatre in their prime, he says, were really something else:

'This was idiosyncratic, aggressive, disturbing, preposterous, ugly stuff — form and content locked in one semi-coherent outburst of violent energy. We were proto-punks, fueled by a set of Situationist slogans - 'What are you against?' 'What have you got?'

If we'd been able to play guitars, we would have formed a band; instead we made physical theatre. It was our only option: arrogance, bad attitude, disrespect for theatre tradition and confrontation with audiences — theatre as traffic accident.'

A little later in his 'archaeological' search, Pearson discovers, in a battered green suitcase in his attic, a sheaf of yellowed A4 sheets with 'Mickery Reviews'. One is entitled, *Ritsaert ten Cate's Justification* in which 'Cate' writes:

RAT Theatre, Newcastle, is a completely new and unexpected star in the English 'Fringe' firmament… Instead of perfectly rehearsed shadow fights, the phenomenon of a group who literally attacked each other with sticks and clubs, had never been seen before and was received with mixed feelings… most had to be satisfied with the admission that they did not know what it was all about, but that it had made a great impression.'

Addendum to the Post Script:

Digging around in my files, at an even later date, I came across the Curriculum Vitae of Pete Sykes. Written when he was 38 years old and presumably given to me, as additional material, to the audio tapes mentioned above.

A number of things strike me about Pete's CV. To begin with, I should mention, as an addition to the opening of the essay above, it appears that RAT had performed in the *Sunday Times* National Student Drama Festival not only in 1971 but in the previous year with a show called *Vietrock*.

Also, although I knew he and RAT had been a touring company from the start, I'm struck by quite how 'international' they had been, in their early years. Pete was obviously proud of this as he foregrounds it on the CV. In their first five years they had toured, and held workshop and training programmes, in Zagreb, Belgrade, Ljubljana, Nancy, Lyon, Turin, Edinburgh, Rome, Milan, Amsterdam, Kiel, Knokke and in later years would develop connections in Skyros and Athens (where the audio tape had been made).

His list of shows created, scripted or devised, also expands on those noted in the essay. So, along with *Hunchback, Blindfold, Judas, The Boy's Own Story* and *Suit of Lights*, there are: *Fifty/50, Reflexions, The Ladder Gang, Inside Out, Assassin, King of a Rainy Country* and numerous other Beckett pieces. There are also 'Music theatre productions' with composer Robert Briggs,

Lorelei and *Visions,* plus the children's plays: *Frisbee Kid, The Adventures of Sidney, Hatrack, Billy and the Toymakers, The Giant Fairy Tale, The Litterbugs of Junk Street, The Water Watchers, Rot, No Buts, Potters Holiday, Folk Tales I & II* and *Doris Dancing.*

All of which, I think, indicates that RAT were an industrious and far reaching company that must have left many audiences and young actors, like myself, with vivid memories of seeing and working with a fantastic theatre company.

As an individual he was *uber* energetic and dynamic, often running workshops on juggling, stilt walking, fire eating, Tai Chi, mime, improvisation, voice work and of course theatre skills. The odd bits of TV he mentions include: *Omnibus* (BBC), *Dream on the Hill* (Granada), *In Celebration* (Granada), *Muck and Brass* (Central/Channel 4), *Crossroads* (Central), *Friday Night and Saturday Morning* (BBC2) and *The Krypton Factor* (Granada).

The last of which, was a very popular TV show on British television, ran for 18 years and was a show in which contestants were put through a battery of physical stamina and mental agility tests.

I recall, now, that Pete told me he'd been on the programme, and had thoroughly enjoyed himself. I can imagine it was just the kind of challenge he relished. I have forgotten exactly how he fared but I'm sure he excelled, as he did in most things he attempted. To my young eyes (and still to the adult) he appeared and was, to use an overused and often too easily applied phrase, 'a real force of nature'. In Pete's case, rather than hyperbole, that was an accurate description of the man.

Artaud

Originally published in PAN Magazine (Spring Edition, no.9, 1999)

Every now and then, we come across an event in history we've never heard of before, an author we never knew existed, a painting never previously pictured in our mind's eye. We experience that sheer delight of something new brightening the eye, giving that old, tired, cynical self a slap in the face and it wakes you up to life again. This happened to me, when I first heard the name Antonin Artaud, seven or so years ago.

I was studying 'A' level Theatre Studies, which meant then (and now): Brecht and *Verfremdung*, Stan- (the-man) -islavki and some crazy French fucker called Antonin Artaud. The expletive by the way, when it comes to Artaud, is not entirely gratuitous, but quite apposite. Artaud is not quite Henry Miller in his lewdness but one of his most famous quotes was, *'All writing is pigshit'* which gives you a flavour of his style. Half-baked, romantic notions of this man then, gently heated my thoughts; fragmentary images really, of someone who was a theatrical explosive. However, I never really got to grips with him during the course: too diffuse, too chaotic, too difficult to handle 'correctly' under the examiner's eye, I guess.

So, for years now, I'd known an interesting little, about the man, a few photographic images occasionally drifted into view, the odd drawing, a phrase or two (*'Theatre should be like a bolt of lightning from a clear blue sky'*). Mild reminders, hints of colour and texture, brushstrokes, rather than a full portrait. That was all I knew. Then one evening, last October, just before setting off to attend one of my regular workshops with Bare Bones Theatre Company, I came across a few rudimentary ideas I'd once had, about doing a play on Artaud's life. The ideas were written on a couple of scraps of paper that had been shoved in the proverbial bottom drawer.

Perhaps it was more conscious that this but that

night happened to be, the night that theatre companies, occasionally, need. The *What is our next project?'* night. The fire was rekindled and so I presented the idea, from my scribbled notes, about a biographical play on Artaud. In its very raw state and with only a little impromptu elaboration on my part, the company agreed - with daunting alacrity - that this should be the next play we put on and I should be its author.

Thus a vague, seven year old idea, on which I thought the dust had settled for good, started its growing pains anew. As I write, this child of chaos has become an unruly teenager and it's more than possible it will soon appear as a fully grown, thoughtful adult. The play is, in other words, written. Our aim is, basically, to convey Artaud's life. So, it's a theatrical biography but his life is to be presented using the style of theatre and theoretical practices he proposed.

This is almost certainly impossible.

During his life time almost all his experiments in theatre failed. His infamous 'Theatre of Cruelty' culminated in a desperate financial, emotional and artistic failure, with the production, in 1935, of his adaptation of Shelley's play *The Cenci*. It's probably true to say Artaud never realized, or transferred successfully, his own theoretical ideas into living theatre. In England, it was left to the likes of Peter Brook and Charles Marowitz, with their 1964 season of the 'Theatre of Cruelty', to produce and 'translate' his theoretical writing, at least somewhat successfully, onto stage.

Clive Barker of Theatre de Complicite wrote of that season:

'Looking back, 1964 can be seen as a crucial crossroads in the British theatre, and the interest in Artaud and Theatre of Cruelty one of the manifestations of a growing frustration with the British actor's inability or unwillingness to physicalize the action rather than intellectualize and verbalize it'

But importantly he adds:

'The Theatre of Cruelty season seems in retrospect to sum up Brook's frustration at being unable to realize his ideas in the British theatre. Subsequent writers, who in the main never saw the performances, have tended to mark down the season as a great success, instead of the

dismal failure I thought it.' (*New Theatre Quarterly*, Vol. 12, issue 46, 1996).

However, the season did produce a legacy as two acting schools, *East 15* and *Drama Centre*, were formed in its wake.

Rather curiously, because initially rather unawares, Bare Bones, as a company, has been uncovering the work of one of its theatrical forebears. Bare Bones dabbled in various forms of theatre over the years, even stretching to a bit of Chekov on occasion. From the start, however, we have located ourselves in the tradition of 'Physical Theatre' – inspired by (and sometimes depressed by the brilliance of) contemporary practitioners such as Volcano, Hoi Poloi and Frantic Assembly. The one advantage of being an amateur company is that our direction or choice of material has never been based on some commercial notion of what 'people' will like but rather what we like and love and are interested in. The implication here is *not* that the companies that have inspired us, are part of commercial theatre, *rather* that we had the luxury of not having to endlessly search for funding, whilst being hard-up actors. Many of the finest actors, of this country, struggle financially their whole career because they do not pursue the more lucrative routes to success. Their success lives in the heart and memory of thousands of people but is largely overlooked by the mainstream media.

That physical 'bent' has unwritten all Bare Bones projects and we have, as I say, almost without knowing it 'received a tradition', the source and history of which we were largely ignorant or unaware of. The concern with the 'physical', and with the 'body', as not just a vocal box delivering text, is one of the most tangible ideas Artaud promulgated during his life. It is an idea which has, one way or another, filtered very broadly into European theatre of the latter end of the 20th century.

In a number of respects our rendition of his life and work will contravene his polemical stance. Artaud's desire was to, somehow, metaphysically create a resonance within his audience, to create in them, the agony it is to be alive. Our more modest aim is to try and capture some of the 'fire within' that drove him to want to obliterate the status quo (within theatre) and burn the texts which have become accepted and canonical. The play offers too much, in the way of the psychological and the biographical, for Artaud to have ever found it acceptable.

Whether our experiment succeeds (and on who's terms anyway?) we will have to wait and see. Nonetheless, we continue in this production and hopefully in future shows, to try and expand our knowledge and deepen our own experience of what theatre is and can be.

Just like life, the work isn't finished and what rehearsal you have, seems to vanish all too quickly.

An Introduction to Artaud

The following is the introduction to my play The Life and Theatre of Antonin Artaud, *retitled and updated from the original (described in the previous essay) which was called* Pigshit.

Sometime, during my undergraduate years, I wrote on an old envelope:

You sit to watch a play. Of what does a play consist? For the Occidental audience, primarily, words. Words that portray the depths of psychological tension of one sort or another: hate, self-loathing, incest, love, the lack of it. But the organisms that sit before me, what, I ask, do you expect tonight? Now? (Pause) In the centre of your head, what have you decided tonight's performance ideally would be and what do you expect? Antonin expects, you *expect, only words. Psychological exposition of intellectual thought, rendered by the spoken but for him somehow pallid, febrile word. Artaud prefers cadence, liturgies, chants, intonations of rhythm, the metaphysical resonance of sound, music, vibration. The vibration of the air, the earth, that will make the coiled snake uncoil and rise and sway, enchanted by the music of its human captor.*

This, as I imagined it, was a monologue from the mouth of Antonin Artaud, author of *The Theatre and Its Double*, which is composed of two manifestoes outlining his belief in a Theatre of Cruelty as he named it. Quite why at the time I was thinking about Artaud, as a character in a play I might one day write, I no longer recall. It was, in fact, almost seven years before an opportunity arose to write the play and the idea bore fruit.

Having performed in many plays, as a teenager, I continued to take acting seriously at university. I played a number of challenging roles in student productions, such as, the vodka drinking, northerner Scullery, in *Road,* by Jim Cartwright and the troubled, Alan Strang, who blinds horses in Peter Shaffer's *Equus.* I also worked, briefly, with Philip Osment, from Gay Sweatshop, on a production of *This Island's Mine,* playing multiple roles including that of Prospero. But really my life had shifted focus, away from theatre and I was immersed in the deep intellectual challenge and excitement of a degree in philosophy. I guess I must have had a moment's inspiration in the canteen or perhaps whilst watching Abel Gance's silent epic, *Napoleon* (in which Artaud features), in the university library. I had certainly scribbled the speech on the first thing that came to hand. I definitely don't recall re-reading at the time anything by the enigmatic, half-crazed, French playwright, whom I'd first come across at school.

In the Sixth Forms of England, during the eighties, if you were a drama student, as I was, and fortunate enough to be on the right syllabus, there were three major theatre practitioners one studied: Constantin Stanislavski, Berthold Brecht and Antonin Artaud.

Stanislavski (or Stan-the-Man as we irreverently

called him) the Russian actor and theatre director, who headed the Moscow Art Theatre and worked closely with Anton Chekhov, seemed (to us precocious teenagers) rather obvious, straight forward and a little boring. We were a generation more than a little used to the idea of 'Method' acting, usually, via the Hollywood films of Marlon Brando and Montgomery Clift. No doubt, we were either ignorant of (or unimpressed by) the fact that such passionate ideas, about acting, had been imported from Stanislavski to America, via such people as Cheryl Crawford and Elia Kazan at The Group Theatre or Lee Strasberg and The Actor's Studio.

Stanislavski's *theory* of an actor utilizing their 'emotional memory', to help create and play a role, was by the time I arrived fresh-faced into a drama studio, not so much assumed, as implicit, so much so, that it hardly seemed worth mentioning or discussing very much as a *practice*. This, no doubt, had once been revolutionary. Stanislavski was really the first person to treat theatre-making seriously, not only as a craft to learn but to be theorized about. Nonetheless, to our youthful ears it was *'old hat'*.

Brecht was more interesting, charismatic, awkward; a firebrand and a Marxist, so likely, in some respects, to appeal to the young. I liked (and still like) his poetry perhaps more than his plays. His theoretical notion of *verfremdungseffekt* or the 'alienation effect' - which entailed constantly breaking an audience's emotional identification with the characters and thus 'alienating' them, so as to more clearly put the playwright's polemic across - whilst intriguing and worth learning, once again, seemed altogether from a different era and intended for a more politically endangered or engaged society than my own.

Artaud? Artaud was the exception. Always the exception, one expects, given his painful, combative, drug filled life of poor health, mental breakdowns and early death at 51. His ideas were rather glossed over by our head of drama, Roy Nevitt, who was excellent and inspirational, in so many other ways, I hesitate to denigrate him on this minor point. In Roy's defence, Artaud is not exactly the most accessible or even coherent of thinkers and, in fact, courted and encouraged an aura of mystery, madness and chaos with relation to his work. Artaud is certainly not your standard high school student's idea of an easy read, so perhaps, the idea was to give him a wide berth generally and let those of us so inclined rediscover him at a more appropriate age.

One example, of Roy Nevitt's exceptional quality as a teacher, was his promulgation of the ideas of Grotowski, in a manner rare in schools (even now I should think). He always treated his students as adults, giving them independence and advice in equal measure, he often left the theatre or drama studio, once he'd instructed us in what we were to do, which inspired confidence and self-reliance. In today's climate that might be seen as a form of neglect but actually it was deeply empowering for his students, who grew in confidence no end. He would crack the flint, scatter the sparks in our adolescent minds and then depart and allow us to imagine, re-imagine and re-engineer the great works we were dealing with. I recall he was passionate about Grotowski's book, *Towards a*

Poor Theatre, which I have to confess, I never read completely, though I was intrigued and fascinated by the photographs between its covers of the obviously intense theatrical experimentation. In my edition of the book there were black and white photos from productions called *Akropolis* and *Dr Faustus* but by far the most striking were the images of Rysared Cieslak in *The Constant Prince* (adapted from Calderón). These images have stayed with me for years and show, without doubt, the utter physical and mental commitment Grotowski sought and received from his actors.

Many years later, I was surprised and delighted to instantly recognize the spirit of Grotowski, before his name was mentioned, and of how transformative his work could be for an actor, whilst watching *My Dinner with André* by Louis Malle. This is perhaps the best rendition of an inspired, meandering, intellectual and quirky conversation that I've ever seen on film. The movie depicts a single conversation, between André Gregory and Wally Shawn (both of whom use their real names), in the Café des Artistes in New York. André abandoned his career, as a successful theatre director, five years ago and since then has been on a personal odyssey, the details of which he recounts to the more skeptical and pragmatic, Wally This journey has seen André experience a string of spiritual awakenings, from being buried alive, as a piece of performance art in Long Island, to mystical and magical encounters in the Sahara and the hippy-ish community at Findhorn, a sixties inspired ecovillage in Scotland. Grotowski is mentioned as part of this five year odyssey, André having, at some point, taken part in a strange theatrical experiment, in a forest, in Poland. Just as a footnote to this paragraph: I find echoes in the conversation of *My Dinner with André* and an early scene in *The Life and Theatre of Antonin Artaud*. The scene, *Dialogue of Letters, 1923-4,* is a fractured interchange between the young Artaud and the reserved man of letters, Jacques Riviére, at the *Nouvelle Revue Française*. Riviére is, all the time, trying to temper Artaud's exaggerations and wildness and bring him back to the 'real world'. This is very similar to what is at the heart Wally's concerns about André and the latter's tendency to feel 'flights of fancy' are not that at all but, in fact, something much more concrete. It's a truism to say Art can (and often does) imitate life. However, for Artaud, Art's territory should, by default, exceed or go beyond the confines of mere 'reality' and the, so called, 'feet-on-the ground' kind of life, that Wally wants to remain upon.

Grotowski's work has a number of similarities to Artaud's but is much more ordered and straight forwardly rational. In the early eighties I worked with RAT Theatre, early interpreters of Grotowski's work in England and early exponents of what is now, generally, called Physical Theatre. Their director, at that time, was Pete Sykes. Pete was an awe inspiring actor not dissimilar to Rysared Cieslak in physique or I imagine in general intensity. I once saw Pete perform Beckett's, *Act Without Words I,* the action of which takes place in a desert and begins with the actor entering *'flung backwards'.* Pete did this *'flung backwards'* as a kind of arching somersault and landed absolutely flat on his back with a loud thwack. The character hears a whistle from off stage right and as

Beckett says: '*…takes the sound for some kind of call, and after a bit of reflection, proceeds in that direction only to find himself hurled back again. Next the sound issues from the left. The scene is repeated in reverse*'.

Whatever is indicated, as following next in the script, in my memory, I recall Pete doing this intense and painful looking action again and again and again. Apparently, he did this without harm and certainly he made it look effortless but the physical prowess it required, I now realize, indicated an actor extremely dedicated to his art. Sadly, Pete died some years ago, I don't know in what circumstances but from personal experience (he once put me up for a couple of weeks), I know he was also an awesome drinker. He appeared to drink dark, heavy pints of Guinness, as if they were water and expected you to do the same!

Before I worked with him (he gave me my first ever acting job) I had the privilege of creating a show with him (and RAT Theatre), as part of a summer project, initiated by Roy Nevitt. That show, *Day Trip to Troy,* I now see, had all kind of influences deeply woven into it. It certainly included elements from Artaud's Theatre of Cruelty and traces of Grotowski's, so called, Theatre Laboratory. It was a crazy, extremely exhilarating summer. We spent many days working extremely hard both physically and mentally: improvising and playing games which expanded our sensory awareness: such as blindfold tag, diving from heights into other actors arms, scouting over fields and rubble barefoot in imitation of tribal practices or wrapping ourselves in large sheets of paper, as 'statues', (so as to, in performance, burst out unexpectedly upon the audience), learning all manner of vocal chants and song and having, it has to be said, a host of other strange and often almost ecstatic moments.

I later interviewed Pete about his career and theories of theatre, for a dissertation. I will always remember, how he put a very particular twist on a number of phrases. Especially the weight he gave to the words, *'The Theatr Laboratorium of Grotowski'*. The colour he put behind those words has not only indelibly stained tracts of my grey matter, it has also always acted as a careful reminder of how ordered, disciplined and scientific, Grotowski's approach was said to be towards acting. In that respect, nothing could be further from the spirit of Artaud, the knowing irrationalist, who was happy to dabble in the occult and opium and, if anything, enjoyed escaping the restraints of the rational. Nonetheless, if one listens to quotes from Grotowski, one hears undoubted echoes of Artaud:

> *The rhythm of life, in modern civilization, is characterized by pace, tension, a feeling of doom, the wish to hide our personal motives and the assumption of a variety of roles and masks in life.*

or

> *Theatre - through the actor's technique, his art in which the living organism strives for higher motives - provides an opportunity for what could be called integration, the discarding of masks, the revealing of the real substance: a totality of physical and mental reactions.*

And again,

It is true that the actor accomplishes this act, but he can only do so through an encounter with the spectator.

The idea of tearing away the masks of civilization and the need to encounter and affect the audience, in a two way process, is central to Artaud's endeavour. Artaud's book, *The Theatre and Its Double* and the notion of the Theatre of Cruelty, seemed, to that teenager of my youth, compellingly visceral. Artaud struck hidden notes, far beyond the personal or political aims of Stanislavski and Brecht. This awkward, cantankerous individual, so full of fire and melancholic *joie de vivre*, was a nihilist, an existentialist, a surrealist, a madman but one who wanted to create an entirely new way of communicating. Errors and false steps were inevitable and a kind of Nietzschean experimentation, to find our *Übermensch*, was bound to include pain. Artaud's notion of Cruelty was not, however, the kind of cruelty that de Sade spoke of semi-philosophically. This Cruelty may have included pain but it was not a Sadism. It was rather a kind of physical (theatrical) violence that sought to shatter form with chaos, rip off false masks, so as to see reality in the flesh. He thought the language, the words, the text (and in this he was a precursor or compatriot of many French thinkers, such as, Bataille, Bartes, Foucault and Derrida), betrayed one; was a dictator to be overthrown.

Theatre, for Artaud, needed a language of its own, halfway between vocal utterance and physical gesture. This was prepared for or enhanced by disturbing theatrical effects: lighting, sound and physical effects were 'thrust' at an audience, in order to startle and shake them out of themselves. Rather than create an alienation or distancing effect, as in Brechtian drama, Artaud wanted the audience to be thrust into the middle of a mêlée or maelstrom of spectacle, so as to shock both the body and mind of the spectator. Much of Artaud's imagery concerns the body, especially the diseased body. Disease and corrupted flesh is a metaphor, a symbol, a true picture of our existence and one of the realities to be cleansed. His drive to create theatre, a form which plays with our notions of what is real, was in part, driven or sustained by his belief in the idea that dreams, nightmares, ecstatic visions and the like, are no less 'real' than the phenomena of everyday existence.

Over the course of my life in theatre, I've had many occasions when I've realized that the project I'm engaged in has been influenced, often unknowingly, but usually positively, by Artaud. *Marat/Sade,* by Peter Weiss, uses the device of a play within a play and is set within the confines of the lunatic asylum at Charenton. The asylum director, Coulmier, tries to help his patient, the Marquis de Sade, by allowing him creative freedom, specifically, the staging of a play, with chaotic results - a situation not so dissimilar to Artaud at the psychiatric hospital, in Rodez, under the treatment of Dr Ferdière.

I once played the part of the Marquis de Sade in the *Marat/Sade* and have watched a number of renditions of the play: at the National, the Bristol Old Vic and several student productions. However, it is still the first production (in English), Peter Brook's for the RSC (made into a film in 1967), that seems the most striking and useful. This was a project that came about after a series of workshops which Brook had run and in which he took as his inspiration Artaud and the Theatre of Cruelty. Incidentally, *Marat/Sade* is a play with music and song but these do not make it a musical in the traditional sense. Weiss employs song, not to advance the narrative, but rather to produce a *verfremdungseffekt,* which shows how theatrical theory constantly spreads, is reinvented and often cross pollinated with other traditions and theories.

Artaud himself got his first inklings of a new type of theatre for the West, at the Paris Colonial Exhibition of 1931, where he saw a company of Balinese dancers perform. This performance prompted an article in the *Nouvelle Revue Française* and seven years later the publication of *The Theatre and Its Double*.

Looking back, over this short introduction, I see how easy it is to make connections between his work and more contemporary trends. Ronald Hayman, in his book on Artaud, written in the seventies, felt he was perhaps the greatest figure of the theatre in the post-war era and cites the names of Beckett, Barrault, Brook, Grotowski and even R.D. Laing as having been deeply influenced by him. Artaud's standing has waned a little since then and he will, I think, always remain a little bit of an outsider to the main stream. However, from the constituency of those passionate about ideas and theatre, he will also always attract readers and draw spectators. The difficulty, since his death, has been the impossibility of knowing whether he would have approved of much of what has followed in his wake.

This play about his life was intended, primarily, as a biographical sketch, to be performed using the techniques of the Theatre of Cruelty. It is likely the biographical narrative of the play is something he himself would have rejected as too psychological, too rational. The Theatre of Cruelty acted as a catalyst to many other types of theatre. It was an ideal and perhaps not an achievable one but it is, I believe, one worth pursuing for the fruits it knocks out of the trees. The text will, as Artaud insisted, always betray one. A new paradigm of expression, his ideas for the Theatre of Cruelty, were something even he believed, at times, *not* possible. As he once wrote to Jean Paulhan:

> *The Theatre I wanted to create presupposed a different form of civilization.*

In the end, it is as Hayman quotes Foucault as saying, *against* the excesses of Artaud, that the world needs to measure itself. Perhaps, it is in such extremis, that we express our humanity most profoundly.

Ophelia

Ophelia *by Bryony Lavery, premiered at Stantonbury Theatre, Milton Keynes, from, 21ˢᵗ to the 30ᵗʰ of November, 1996. The review below was originally published, in the short lived publication on the performing arts,* PAN Magazine *(Winter Edition, no.2, 1997).*

Bryony Lavery is a Yorkshire born dramatist, best known for her award winning play Frozen *(1998), about a serial killer, which premiered at Birmingham Rep and then transferred to the Cottesloe Theatre at the National.* Frozen *was also nominated for four Tony Awards, in 2004, having transferred to Broadway. Lavery has also written five plays for the National Theatre's annual youth theatre scheme the* Connection Series, *many BBC Radio adaptations and also authored translations of foreign plays, such as,* Uncle Vanya *by Chekov.*

The performance of her play Ophelia, *at a low key venue in Milton Keynes, was, I suspect, a 'try out' and in all likelihood was rewritten later in its life. I knew nothing of her reputation at the time and because I knew several people connected to the production I may well have assumed Lavery was a local playwright. Although I was in my early thirties, I was nonetheless, as a putative theatre critic, as green as they come. Lavery, as one time Artistic Director of Gay Sweatshop and a founder of the feminist cabaret group,* Female Trouble, *intended the play as a feminist critique (on Shakespeare if nothing else) but it was obviously too subtle, weak and/or I, too naïve, to appreciate the fact.*

This adaptation of *Hamlet* essentially lacked teeth. In a sea of troubles there were, however, islands of respite. The first of these atolls was Bryony Lavery's language which, although it often got lost in the sheer elephantine size of this production, did occasionally glisten through.

A central question raised by this text, which included some of Shakespeare's most explosive female characters, was why adapt *Hamlet* anyway? Presumably, the idea was to let us delve into the psychology of these characters, in a way Shakespeare never allowed? However, apart from Ophelia (and Gertrude perhaps) very little of the play's dramatic canvas was given over to these 'new' characters, whose fleeting appearances seemed more like cameos than psychological portraits of any depth. I had half expected a feminist piece but unhappily the play never even came near to that.

Our eponymous heroine, as if by a process of *pentimento*, only gradually appeared and in this version of the story is more erudite and self-assured than the ever vacillating Great Dane. But although Kate Ankers, as Ophelia, played the part well, there was still too much residue from the original – who all too easily dives into a scented insanity – for this Ophelia to ever take flight.

Lady Katherina, Lady Macbeth, Goneril, Portia, Lady Capulet (and servants), all appeared, later than one might have expected, dressed uniformly, in striking costumes of mourning.

Unfortunately, 'wheeled on' might be a clearer, touch exaggerated, description because apart from complaining about their rooms in Elsinore, the actors were given little opportunity to show us the character that each had obviously developed in the workshop stage of the production. Despite this, I thought, Wendy Mertens especially good as a gently eloquent Lady Capulet.

One interesting and surprising element of the adaptation was that Gertrude was recast as slightly more villainous than in the original and one almost felt sympathy for, of all people, her new husband, Claudius. But such touches were the exception.

The male actors, in general, seemed to me either miscast, overplayed or misdirected. Oscar Sharp, as Hamlet and Will Swann as an incestuous Laertes, both needed, I felt, to play their roles with greater inner depth and less external passion.

For me at least, although a great deal of time and money obviously went into this venture, any narrative tension that may lie within the play, was overburdened by overproduction and, in the end, the show lacked dramatic bite.

The Treatment

The premiere of The Treatment *by Ursula White and Catapult Theatre was performed at the Madcap Theatre, in Wolverton. Once again, I was the reviewer for* PAN Magazine *(Winter Edition, No.8, 1998).*

If what you want from an evening is Entertainment, this well-crafted play gave you entertainment, with a big 'E'. Many, of this all too small an audience, laughed heartily throughout the show. A few, such as myself, laughed less but that was really a question of personal preference, with relation to the genre of the play itself. This was a bit of a *Carry On*. Less childish and certainly less sexist, whilst still clinging tightly on, to its innuendo.

This young crew of three actors beat the 'tempo' of farce at just the right pace. The physical antics, of both cast and set, were very well rehearsed and fell into place every time. Timing, delivery and quality of dialogue were all tight and well-handled but whilst there was a tangential political point (about the contemporary evil of Government Audit and hospital cuts) this was much too slight to provoke serious analysis. If the satirical elements of the play worked at all, it was in relation to our subjective natures and foibles rather than our societal idiocies.

I have the misfortune, in a sense, of reviewing a play that I felt to be of a much higher quality than the company's first production, both in terms of its acting and writing. *'The misfortune'* being that comedy generally and this kind of British farce, in particular, are mostly not my cup of tea.

Yet, even so, I thought the play and its performance well accomplished. I would happily recommend *The Treatment* to anyone who is a fan of this type of show because, especially with a large audience belly-laughing away, you would not be disappointed.

Personally, I admired many aspects of the dialogue and the overall structuring of the play, which was very neat and effective. The subject matter was a bit 'old hat' at times – jolly japes in a hospital – but the idea of someone impersonating a doctor, treating someone who wants to be ill but isn't and then these two characters falling for each other, literally at times, worked very well and never seemed to be out of control (or ludicrous) within the dynamic and internal logic of *The Treatment*.

Ted Hughes Meets Sylvia Plath

Fragment of an incomplete play

Note: Lines not in italics are spoken as narration

Ted: Where was it? In the Strand? A display of news items? In photographs? For some reason I noticed it. A picture of that year's intake of Fulbright scholars. Just arriving or arrived, or some of them. Were you among them? Was it then I bought a peach? It was the first peach I'd ever tasted. I could hardly believe how delicious it was. Twenty five, dumbfounded I was, dumbfounded by my ignorance at the simplest things.

That photo. I studied it, not too minutely, wondering which of them I might meet. I remember that thought. Not your face.

No doubt I scanned particularly the girls.

Maybe I noticed you, maybe weighted you up, feeling unlikely. Noted your long hair, loose waves, your Veronica Lake bang. Not what it hid. And your grin, your exaggerated American grin, for the cameras. Then I forgot.

Yet, I remember the picture: the Fulbright Scholars. With their luggage? Seems unlikely. Did they come as a team?

Someone's girlfriend shared a supervisor and a weekly session with you. Lucas' American girlfriend that's right, she detested you. But Lucas became your friend anyway. I was still slogging away in an office near slough, hoarding my wages so I could fund my leap to freedom: university. And he was there with you, *knew* you. I heard of it and was fed snapshots, neither of them realized how inflammable that celluloid was to me.

Lucas: *Are you sure?*

Ted: *Don't be such a silk shirt!*

Ted: We were drunk, it was midnight.

Lucas: *What time is it?*

Ted: *Christ, I dunno. Ouch, bloody rose bushes!*

Lucas: *It's that one up there.*

Ted: *Which one?*

Lucas: *The one in the middle.*

Ted: *Are you sure?*

Lucas: *Yes, I'm bloody sure. Now, come on, fancy pants!*

Ted: *What?*

[Lucas begins throwing stones up at a window above, Ted joins in]

Ted: He was certain it was yours. I didn't know. Nor did I know I was being auditioned. That I was to be the lead actor, in your drama. The male lead, in the starry darkness and the shadow, unknown to you and not knowing you. There I was, miming the first easy movements, feeling for the role, as if…

[From a window above]

Voice: *Oi, you pair of college tossers, piss off!*

Ted: It was the wrong window.

***

Ted: According to Prospero's book it was a bad night for a party. Jupiter and the full moon were in conjunction. Venus was pinned exactly on my mid-heaven. It was freshmen days and we wanted to launch our magazine with a literary splash and if you wanted, a future Chaucer or Dante to hob-nob, you needed to spend a lot of cash and to make it look good, elegant, expensive.

[Loud music: Joe Lyde, Jazz]

Lucas: *Quite a buffet you have out there old kid, must have cost a packet?*

Ted: *Hardly, but they've made a nice job of it.*

Lucas: *Yes, they have. What's the music? Makes me feel I'm about to go overboard on the Titanic.*

Ted: *What?*

Lucas: *Like the Titanic, [leans over as if going overboard] Whey hey, 'Man overboard!'*

Ted: *What? Yes.*

[The music stops. The action freezes]

Ted: Suddenly, it was like I was in a silent film, as if Gloria Swanson has just swept into our little party. Lucas had engineered it, suddenly, it was you. My first sight, like a snapshot, stilled in the camera's glare. You were taller, taller than you ever were again, perfect American legs that simply went on up.

[Sylvia and Ted dance a jitterbug. They freeze]

Ted: Your eyes, squeezed in your face, a crush of diamonds, incredibly bright.

[They unfreeze, dance, then freeze again]

Ted: Bright as a crush of tears. You meant to knock me out with your vivacity and you did.

[They unfreeze. Ted speaks whilst they dance and then, towards the end, his girlfriend comes forward and intercedes between Ted and Sylvia, dragging Ted away]

Ted: I don't remember much else of that evening, except… my girl-friend, Susan, like a loaded crossbow, waiting nearby, in a corner somewhere. But your face was a tight ball of joy. I see you more clearly, clearer, more *real* than in any of the years that followed and that loose fall of hair, that glamorous fashionable bang, over your face and over your scar. I would grow to realize your face was like the sea, never the same twice. A small stage, for weathers and subtle currents, its scar, like its makers, a deliberate flaw. I remember very little else from that night but when I see your face it's as if I saw you that once, then never again. I recall nothing but the swelling ring-moat of tooth-marks on my cheek and my girlfriend, her hissing rage in a doorway and my stupefied interrogation.

***

Ted: Next was 18 Rugby Street's Victorian squalor. I was waiting for you, Lucas was bringing you. I think of that house as a stage-set. Four floors exposed to the auditorium, the love-struggle in all its acts and scenes; a 'snakes and ladders' of interchanging and disentangling of limbs and lives.

I lived there alone, though there was a Belgian girl in the ground floor flat, plump as a mushroom. She had nothing to do with the rest of the house but play her part in the drama. Her house-jailor, who kept her in solitary, was a demon: a highly explosive, insane, black Alsatian that challenged, through the chained crack of the door, every entrance and exit. He guarded her, but not from her gas-oven, seven years into the future. She was nothing to do with me.

I sat alone at the hacked, archaic, joiner's bench that did for a desk and table. I waited. Happy to be martyred for folly, I invoked you; bribing Fate to produce you.

Lucas: *Come on. We call it the Eagles Nest… actually, I call it the Vulture's Lair. Ted should be there.*

Sylvia: *I'm in London. Just for the night. I need to catch the train early tomorrow morning.*

Ted: I can hear you, babbling, to be overheard, breathless.

Sylvia: *Paris, in April, is supposed to be fabulous…*

Ted: Climbing the bare stairs…

Sylvia: But I'm not sure…

Ted: Alive and close. *[They arrive and knock on Ted's door. As he speaks, he answers the door and lets Sylvia in. Lucas is left outside]* That was your artillery, to confuse me, before coming over the top in your panoply, you wanted me to hear your panting. Then, blank. How did you enter? What came next? How did Lucas delete himself?

Sylvia: And now at last…

Sylvia: I got a good look at you.

Ted: Your roundy face that…

Sylvia: …Your friends…

Ted: …being objective…

Sylvia: …called 'rubbery' and you…

Ted: …crueler…

Sylvia: … 'boneless'.

Ted: A spirit mask…

Sylvia: …in its own séance.

Ted: And I became aware of the mystery of…

Ted: …your lips.

Sylvia: You…

Sylvia: …like nothing before in my life.

Ted: …Their aboriginal thickness…

Sylvia: *Your nose…*

Ted: …Broad and Apache…

Sylvia: *…Nearly a boxer's nose.*

Ted: That made every camera your enemy. *[Pause]* Your worship needed a god. You were pausing, a night in London before your escape to Paris, April 13th. Your father's birthday. Your Daddy had been aiming you at God, when his death touched the trigger. You saw your whole life, it ricocheted, the length of your

Alpha career with the fury of…

Sylvia: *A high-velocity bullet…*

Ted: *…That cannot shed one foot-pound of kinetic energy.*

Ted: Later, I learned the desperation of that
search, scattering your tears around the
cobbles of Paris; the dream you hunted
for; the life you begged to be given again

I guessed you were off to whirl through
some euphoric American Europe. Under
your hair, done this way and done that
way, the cascade of cries diminuendo,
you were gold-jacketed, solid silver,
nickel tipped. Your real target hid behind
me. The God with the smoking gun. I
did not even know I had been hit or that
you had gone clean through me, to bury
yourself, at last, in the heart of the god.
In my position, the right witchdoctor
might have caught you in flight with his

bare hands. Tossed you, cooling, one hand to the other, Godless, happy, quieted. I managed a wisp of your hair, your ring, your watch, your nightgown. But now, you declaimed a long poem about a panther.

Sylvia: While I held you and kissed you.

Ted: I tried to keep you from flying about the room. For all that you would not stay. We walked south across London to Fetter Lane and your hotel… in the roar of your soul your scar told me how you had tried to kill yourself. And I heard…

Sylvia: Opposite the entrance, on a bombsite becoming a building site, we clutched each other giddily, for safety, and went in a barrel together, over some Niagara Falls.

Ted: Falling, in the roar of your soul, your scar told me how you had tried to kill yourself. And I heard…

Sylvia: Without ceasing for a moment to kiss…

Ted: …You. As if, a sober star whispered it, above the rumbling city.

Sylvia: Stay clear.

Ted: How I smuggled myself, wrapped in you, into the hotel, I cannot remember. You were slim and lithe and smooth as a fish. You were a new world, my new world. So, this is America, I marveled. Beautiful, beautiful America!

***

[Sylvia is frozen in a dance move. Ted moves about her, as if she were a statue in an art gallery]

Ted: Nobody wanted your dance. The dark ate at you. The grinding indifference. And there it was too, the mystery of hatred. Whilst I was sitting in *The Anchor,* just draining my Guinness, you wrote of the *'huge dark machine'.* These words had come to you, when I did not.

Nobody wanted your dance, your strange glitter. Your journal pages, your effort, to cry words; came apart in aired blood, adrenalins of despair, terror, sheer fury. It was a panther that had dragged you across Europe, as if in its jaws, as if trailing between its legs. After forty years, the whiff of that beast, off the dry pages, off your journal, lifts the hair on the back of my hands. Most likely, I was just sitting with Lucas, no more purpose in me than in my own dog (that I did not have) while the grotesque mask of your Mummy-Daddy, half quarry, half-hospital, whole juggernaut, stuffed with your unwritten poems, ground invisibly without a ripple towards me.

Nobody wanted your dance, your floundering, drowning life. You tried your upmost, with gifts of yourself. Just like your first words as a toddler, when you rushed at every visitor, clasping their legs and crying *'I love you, I love you!'*. Just as you danced, for your father, in the home of anger.

Gifts of your life, to sweeten his slow death and mix yourself in it, where he lay, propped on the couch; to sugar the bitterness of his raging death.

Nobody wanted your dance. Your effort to save yourself, treading water, dancing the dark turmoil, looking for something to give. Whatever you gave, they bombarded with splinters, derision, mud... the mystery of that hatred. After your billions of years in anonymous matter, you were found, and promptly, hated

[Sylvia, as Ted turns away, speaks to his back]

Sylvia: *Dying is an art, like everything else. I do it exceptionally well.*

***

[Ted and Sylvia, opposite sides of the stage. Ted, on the train, is reading. Sylvia, at the bus station, is anxious, looking for the bus]

Ted: Because the message somehow met a goblin.

Sylvia: *God damn it to hell. Where are you Ted? Excuse me, sorry to bother you but do you know, is that the 8.10?*

Man: *Dunno, love.*

Sylvia: *Thank you. Excuse me, the bus you just got off, was that the 8.10? Final stop here, Victoria?*

Woman: *Yes.*

Ted: Because precedents tripped your expectations.

Ted: *Excuse me, is this the final stop?*

Passenger: *Dunno, mate. I think so.*

Ted: *Sorry, is this the final stop?*

Ticket collector: *That's right Sir, yes.*

Ted: Because you're London was still a kaleidoscope.

Sylvia: *Well where is he?*

Driver: *I'm sorry, love, I dunno.*

Ted: A kaleidoscope of names and places.

Sylvia: *He's tall, you couldn't miss him. Perhaps you saw him just missing the bus? Just before you pulled away?*

[Sylvia starts to rush, up through the auditorium perhaps]

Ted: You waited, begged the driver to produce me or to remember seeing me. Finally, somebody calmer than you, must have had a suggestion because when I got off the train *[Sylvia is getting closer as he speaks]* expecting to find you, I saw a figure breasting the flow of released passengers, your molten face, your molten eyes *[they embrace]* your flinging arms, your scattering tears, as if I'd come back from the dead. There, I knew what it was to be a miracle. And behind you, your taxi-driver, laughing, like a small god, to see an American girl being, so American. Your cross-London panic dash, and now your triumph. It was a wonder that my train was not earlier, even much earlier, that it pulled in late, the very moment you irrupted onto the platform.

Sylvia: *It was natural, and miraculous, and an omen. It confirmed everything. Everything that I wanted confirmed.*

Ted: *Like the first thunder cloudburst, engulfing the drought in August.*

Sylvia: *Like when every leaf trembles and everything holds up its arms, weeping.*

[They say the next lines together]

Ted: *It was a wonder.*

Sylvia: *It was a wonder.*

Can a God Die?

I

During the course of writing, rewriting and editing this volume of essays, I had cause at one point to write on two computers. Somewhere along the line, I rewrote 'Can a God Die?' *twice (without recalling the first rewrite on the alternative computer)!*

So extensive were these rewrites that the two versions whilst covering the same topic, have (apart from a couple of paragraphs) little repeated content. I have therefore elected to keep both in the collection as genuine reflections of my thought on the subject on, separate occasions. And incidentally, to show how writers, like everyone else, work around a subject by refining, redefining and trying out new thoughts. Being the insubstantial, frail creatures that we are, our thoughts are a moveable feast and so, depending what day you arrive, the food on the table inevitably changes.

I am no theologian but with regard to Christianity I have particular theological problems. These are centred round the crucifixion and the death of Christ.

To begin with, I'm quite unsure what to make of the notion of allowing one's 'son' to be murdered. What kind of moral lesson am I supposed to draw from this?

Then there is, of course, the difficult idea of Christ being *not exactly* the son of God, so much as, one third of God. In what sense *can* or if you believe, *did,* Christ-God die? If he had an immortal soul, which even normal human beings are said to have within the belief system, I presume that that did not die? We are then left then with *only* the mortal body dying. Even this corporeal element is 'clocked', a few days after death, having a chat on the road to Emmaus. So, in a sense, neither immortal soul, nor mortal body die or die for very long.

Following on from this, one wonders, can a god (or even a part of a god) die anyway? If an omnipotent God died wouldn't the universe go with him?

There are, of course, a number of gods that have died, mostly in the various pantheistic traditions (of the past and present) but in monotheism that would be problematic if it were a true death, by which I mean a final and absolute death. *[In passing, it's just occurred to me that, given belief in the Trinity (by some Christians at least), technically speaking, perhaps Christianity isn't actually a monotheism anyway?]* Certainly, there are various previous models (of god) who died and were resurrected: Adonis, Dionysus, Krishna, Osiris, and Mithras to name but a few. Other similarities, within this group, include crucifixion, as the means of death, and virgin (or miraculous births) from mortal mothers, along with many other parallel practices and traditions.

Be that as it may, this sort of self-elected, semi-death of Christ's, has always seemed odd to me as a *moral* example i.e. God choosing pain and dying as a means of somehow 'paying' for our sins. What does that mean, *'he died for our sins'*? Surely (given you believe in the concept of sin in the first place) people have continued to sin? So, even if the slate were wiped clean, humanity filled it up again pretty quickly. If Christ didn't die, to *rid* us of our sin, for what reason did he die? To show us we were sinners but that he loved us anyhow?

It is said by believers that we are inherently sinful and we die because Adam and Eve, having been given the freedom to disobey god, did so, and ate from the tree of knowledge of good and evil. Having 'infected' us all with sinfulness and the potential to die, Christ's death somehow heals us and allows us once again eternal life.

> '*He was pierced for our transgressions, he was crushed for our iniquities; the punishment that brought us peace was on him, and by his wounds we are healed.*' (Isiah 53:5)

Christ-God allowed himself to be 'killed' so we, ordinary human beings, could be forgiven? If I have this right, my ancestors, Adam and Eve, do something God says is a sin. God feels, I (along with the rest of humanity) am also to be held guilty (or am tainted somehow) for those actions. He then kills his own son/self to absolve and resolve matters? As I say, I'm not a theologian and perhaps that's the only way you can even begin to understand such logic?

Anyway, Christ suffered, not the most painful, though a quite nasty death, stayed 'dead' for a few days and then returned to his father-self? Again, I don't get it. I honestly think the crucifixion, resurrection (and redemption of humanity) is a very confused and confusing narrative, partially perhaps, because it's rooted in the Judaic and pre-Judaic mind-set i.e. the semi-pagan notion of sacrificing animals to God.

Whilst I understand (to a degree) in *psychological* terms how and why such visceral, emotive and symbolic bloodletting appeals to some, it is certainly is not based on rational thinking.

My points above, are I realize, rather piled up, pell-mell, one atop another and perhaps crudely stated but sophisticated argument here, would to this outsider, feel more like obfuscation. Talk of the 'greater metaphysic' is used intentionally (and unintentionally it seems) to obscure the oddity of the popular narratives and parables within the Christian story.

Of course, why should a Christian be rational? Christianity is a variety of irrationalism, which, in and of itself, may be just as understandable a response to the absurdity of human affairs, as rationalism. It's just hard for me, from my perspective i.e. someone who wants to understand our existence, to really comprehend or relate to such a need for 'mystery' or more accurately 'paradox' and the functional illogicality of Christian Irrationalism. Perhaps it is futile to try?

By definition, irrational belief systems hold that, ontologically, the world is essentially devoid of rational structure, that our reasoning (our epistemic base) is incapable of fully knowing or getting to grips with existence, and the universe, without distortion and that essentially we are built of irrational forces and our only recourse, ethically, is to believe in something outside ourselves. Given that, can you having meaningful dialogue with someone who believes in the Trinity or that a God can die? Faith, is the foundation, not 'true belief in' or understanding of, *the logos* but rather its reification into an incomprehensible unknowable. If 'the Word is God', understanding is beyond words.

Agnosticism is the only position I can accept i.e. accepting that I do not and cannot know the ultimate meaning (or lack of meaning) in the universe. Pascal's wager, of betting on God just in case he exists, seems intellectually dishonest to me (and surely God would recognize, and disapprove of, your gambling ways anyway?).

If I were to be religious, I guess, I'd have to be a Deist of some sort (as my Dad once said he was). That is, I'd have a kind of generalized notion of a God *'out there'* somewhere and *'in who's image'* we were not all that similar. A God, that didn't 'inspire' or write books (which are so open to interpretation) that people regularly murder each other, over the meaning of the contents.

Can a God Die?

II

I am no theologian. However, with regard to Christianity, I have particular theological problems.

Putting aside, the odd idea, that an omnipotent god chooses to communicate his ideas via a book (at least eventually, after decades of retelling and then three centuries of rewrites), my difficulty is centred on the crucifixion and the death of Christ.

To begin with, I'm quite unsure what to make of the notion of allowing one's 'son' to be murdered. What kind of moral lesson am I supposed to draw from this? If I put my child in front of an on-coming bus, so as to be killed, what response should I expect from those who see or hear of the action?

In truth, my problem here is with the Christian attachment to the notion and practice of sacrifice, even though sacrifice is, and has been, a part of many religions. I simply do not understand what it means. I have never understood what ritual killing means. How does the killing of the Christ help me or anybody else exactly?

In the spilling of his blood, in being murdered, his life is said to have been perfected or *'made perfect'* (Hebrews 5:8-9). Jesus, the Christ, is an example of someone who gives his life for others but not quite in the usual way. He is not a Steve Biko, an Ernesto Guevara, a Martin Luther King, an Emily Wilding Davison or a Mohandas Karamchand Gandhi fighting for something specific. It is specifically his *death* that he offers, which is not an unfortunate by-product of his actions, it is their culmination and apogee. His not a martyr or saint but a deity choosing to 'die'. He sacrifices his bodily life to save 'Us'.

To sacrifice can be seen as an offering, an atonement, an act of repentance, a gift, a punishment or a symbol of holiness itself. Actually, in the normal course of things, the Judeo-Christian-Islamic god prefers obedience, to the mere formality of a holocaust or burnt offering (*'To obey is better than sacrifice, and to heed*

is better than the fat of rams.' 1 Samuel 15:22).
Perhaps, for some, my approach may be too
caught up with the literalness of interpretation
but the 'offering up' of one's life, as a gift,
seems to me unpalatable. The self-obsession,
extremism, violence and lack of gentle
philosophy seems wasteful, unnecessary and
fetishistic.

To kill anything, even oneself, doesn't seem to
resolve or atone for much, though, I suppose, it
shows one is serious about repenting or making
one's point, even if it achieves nothing in
practical terms (though the more 'practical'
death of the Crusader or Jihadist seems even
worse).

Of course, the 'atonement' here, is *by* God, for
and with humanity (*'God was in Christ, reconciling
the world to Himself.'* 2 Corinthians 5:19). God
has (attempted) to atone, to become 'at one'
and reconcile himself again, with the human
race. Again, it strikes me just how odd this
sacrifice was. Did he (and the Christian god is
most definitely a 'he') achieve such a
reconciliation? Or was that just for believers?

Has the world benefited from this reconciliation? My questions go on but you see the drift of this unbeliever's vision. I can see the fire through the smoke but not much else.

If the sacrifice were a punishment of some sort, which in the main, my Christian friends assure me it *isn't* but, if it were, that wouldn't achieve a great deal either would it? Or would it? The person who receives 'punishment' (in this case the sinners of the world) experiences pain and suffering and perhaps regret, remorse and existential angst. But those who have suffered his sins (in this case God), only have the cool pleasure of seeing justice exacted (in the remorse of the sinner perhaps?) or the colder comfort of revenge. The initial harm (disappointment or offence) inflicted is not reversed. When God has himself punished, for *our* transgressions, we may wish to bury the memory of those transgressions but we can't un-write our history, though I concede, we may wish to do better next time.

It may make no sense, that Christ has himself murdered or killed for us sinners but so it doesn't happen again (and surely a second crucifixion would negate the whole process) perhaps we should give up being sinners? Though, of course, we were only born sinners, because that's how we were born. That is, Adam and Eve transgressed, we, as individuals, did not! The logic here appears, to this mortal, to be more a muddy puddle than what I presume is the eternal clarity of the waters surrounding God.

If, however, Christ's sacrifice is *not* a punishment, we are left with sacrifice as *'a symbol of holiness itself'*. The sacrifice looked for, to be imitated, is obedience to the laws of God, for people to *'write them on their hearts'* (Hebrews 8:10). Sacrifice, is doing God's will (Hebrews 10:7-9), sacrifice is loving others (Ephesians 5:2), avoiding sin (John 1:29), serving God (Romans 12:1) and praising God (Hebrews 13:15). It turns out sacrifice is many things.

Sacrifice is, as Thomas á Kempis put it, the imitation of Christ. Sacrifice is… really? Again, this seems no more than unthinking, unexamined rhetoric, the transmutation of a word (sacrifice) into something so multifarious, meaning so many things, symbolizing so much, that it can only be comprehended when you leave understanding, logic, plain speaking and common sense behind and replace it with faith. It is a kind of reverse reification where the abstract, becomes concrete (in sacrifice), only to become obscurely abstract once again. In *Mere Christianity*, C.S.Lewis wrote,

> *'The terrible thing, the almost impossible thing, is to hand over your whole self - all your wishes and precautions -to Christ.'*

Indeed, it seems both *'terrible'* and near *'impossible'* to me too. I am, however, being facetious when I say so (Lewis, by the way, is a writer I love. His writing on the medieval period is fascinating, brilliant and second to none).

The other element of the crucifixion I struggle with, in my literalistic way, is the difficult idea of Christ being, not exactly the son of god, so much as, one third of god. The answers given, in response to the question of the Trinity, are labyrinthine but fundamentally Christians want it both ways, Trinity and no Trinity. So, firstly, it will be asserted that whilst there are many names or epithets for god (Jehovah, Jah, Yah, Yahweh, El, El-Shaddai, Elohim, Eloah, Elyon, Lord God Almighty, Adon, Adonai to name but a few) there is only *one* God.

In fact, for a long time, I believed the reasonably common assertion, that in a poly- and pan-theistic world, Christianity was the first monotheism. At some point, my interest in Egyptology led me to discover the Aten, of the Pharaoh Arkenaten, which immediately made me question that 'received idea'. Then, digging deeper, I found Zoroaster's Ahura Mazda, the Babylonian Marduk, Lord Krishna from the Vedic tradition and so on, all of which are monotheisms that predate Christianity. It was not so much an outright falsehood that Christianity was the first monotheism, more that, because it had become so dominant and central to Western tradition, a traditional ignorance of other religions had watered the flower of this untruth.

To return to the Trinity: of Father, Son and

Holy Spirit. I know that if we think of the Hebraic ('*ruach*') and Greek ('*pneuma*') meaning of 'Spirit' we find a closer translation is 'breath' rather than 'spirit' (or 'ghost', as it's also, sometimes, translated). The breath or the spirit of God is easier perhaps to incorporate into the concept of the 'metaphysical', than the Son and the Father. A body without breath is dead, hence the spirit (which is not the soul) comes into the picture. The inanimate 'lives' and is animated when the breath of the divine is breathed into it. The divine wind is immediately more ethereal and metaphysical and it feels almost like a trait or lively characteristic of God. But Father and Son?

Well, of course, one needs to be less, or is it more, literal? A good analogy is actually with human beings, made in the 'image of God' of course. If you think of humans as having an invisible soul, a visible body and an animating spirit, then those three things equate to the Trinity. The Father is the invisible, the Son the visible and the Holy Ghost the animating spirit. Simple, a complex that makes a unity. Yet there is something wrong here. Is the problem of the

Trinity just a question of nomenclature? Ignore the Father/Son language and you're alright? Replace or substitute the traditional terminology, for more conceptually apt terms, and it all settles itself? I don't see that.

Christ acts as a *son* in relation to God. He asks why his father has forsaken him for example. This is dialogue (otherwise it soon becomes parody: If this isn't a son pleading with a father the 'dialogue' becomes a parody e.g. *Why have you, that is I, forsaken me, that is myself?'* etc.).

God, of course, is said to be mysterious and incomprehensible, in certain ways. So, let's just go with, '*God 'is one, with Christ and the Holy Spirit'* for the moment. This being the case, in what sense can or did Christ (third of God that he is) die on the cross? If he had an immortal and eternal soul, as human beings are said to have (and whilst being 'God', he was also said to be human), I presume, if by 'death' one means eternal non-existence, then his soul did not and could not have died. Are we then left with it being *only* the mortal body of Jesus that ceased to function and died?

This corporeal body of his, only dies for a few days of course, before he is up (like Lazarus) and walking again. So, it seems, from my viewpoint at least, that neither immortal soul, nor mortal body, die (or die for very long). Nonetheless, it is still said, Christ *'died for our sins'*, which prompts the further question, *'Can a god die?'*

This semi-death (of Christ's) has always seemed peculiar to me, both as a moral example i.e. a god choosing pain and 'death' to somehow 'pay' for the sins of humanity. And in addition, isn't it just an outright, flat contradiction, that if Jesus was 'resurrected', he *didn't* die did he? Not really, not if 'dead', means eternally 'not living any more'.

Then again, what does it mean, that *'he died for our sins'* as Christians continually repeat? Also, did he just wipe the slate clean for a bit, so we could then carry on as we had before? It's true he suffered, though not the most painful death one can imagine (can't say it's the way I want to go mind you), but he only stayed dead for a few days and then returned to heaven and his father/self didn't he? Where, I presume (I've not been), he still resides

To the surprise of my Christian friends, I honestly find it a very confused and confusing narrative. I understand sacrifice and death cults have a long history and appeal to people and many of the ideas are even pagan and pre-date Judaism and Christianity etc. but, for myself, the psychological appeal is distant. Whilst I find some Irrationalism (Nietzsche's for instance) stimulating and thought provoking, the irrational faith of Christians is too muddled and reliant on paradox, to create faith in me.

Atheistic-leaning-agnosticism seems the only position I can accept i.e. accepting that I do not, and cannot, know the ultimate meaning (or lack of meaning) in the universe. Atheism, while I basically empathize with it, seems to me, to fall into the same absolutism as faith. Atheism, ironically, posits, in one major respect, the same position as faith. Both Atheists and Theists claim a secure and *absolute certainty*. This is a certainty I just don't think we, as human beings, can have.

I *believe* in science, over faith, but it is a belief in Empiricism (which is a moveable feast and rightly so) and Karl Popper's statement, that science is based on potentially refutable hypothesis or what he called 'Falsificationism'. Absolute claims are, by this definition, unscientific in their outlook.

Late in life, my father, who'd only ever expressed atheistic sentiments, told me he was actually a Deist. He'd been reading Thomas Paine's *The Age of Reason* and had concluded he agreed with Tom. *The Age of Reason* has a marvelous polemic which deconstructs Christianity and 'religions of the book'. Basically, Paine's question is simple. Why, he asks, would any omnipotent God bother to communicate via a book?

If I were to be religious, I guess, like my Dad, I'd have to be a Deist of some sort. So Father, Son and Spirit do come together in my life in one way! As a Deist, I'd have a generalized notion of a god 'out there', a natural non-anthropomorphic phenomenon probably. In the unlikely event of this god wishing to communicate, it would seem bizarre for it to do so, via a book centred on crucifixion. Rather, God (who'd also be unlikely to have a gender) would communicate directly, in the form of a mental communication, beamed right into the core of our being. It would be a message, about which we could have no doubts, and which we would not question or dispute. There would be no bloody books with which to inspire murder or entertain apocalypse.

A Very Slight Anticipation

What You Find in Second Hand Books

There is always a very slight anticipation, when you open a second handbook, that there might be an interesting inscription or that a slip of paper may fall out with something mysterious on it. Well, I recently experienced both, whilst browsing in the book section of a charity shop.

Firstly, I picked up a book on Spandau Prison in West Berlin, which held, for many years, seven of the Nazi's top brass, who had been convicted, at the Nuremberg Trials, after the Second World War. They were: Hess, Speer, Dönitz, Raeder, von Schirach, Neurath and Funk – which when you say them aloud makes you feel like you're naming the seven dwarfs (which, in terms of their moral standing, they were in a way)! On the book's flyleaf, I found an inscription, from one of the former prison-guards. Then, picking up a second book, a biography of a Bulgarian Scientist-Inventor (someone I'd never heard of), two sheafs of letter paper, with handwritten notes, fell out. I transcribe what was on the sheafs below:

18:15 E-

Hope you are okay? Got worse over last three days. Only you understand.

11:30 N-

Sod this – being dead can't be worse – she was my life, no-one gets that.

H- replied – Cheeky sod – always here for you

You and her have to get on with your lives – want to come and see you.

H- : She will get on with her life not under my roof.

4th

02:40 She was my life no-one understands he feels [undecipherable word] everything to him.

'You get that?'

5 minutes later

Going to Denby to confront – J

4:30 Therapy on Friday – just don't want to live

No job, friends, confidence

No-one understands.

10:30 Want to hate her

Being dead must be better

No point in anything

8th

Can't cope – last chance of happiness – have no life

All quite dramatic, and I'm sure, if I had a novelist's mind, I would be working out a plot around it right now. *[I am quite certain no one concerned will ever read this but, just in case, I have left only letters for the names of people mentioned]*.

Discovering such oddments often induces a gentle melancholia for some reason. Perhaps, because one feels a sense of how quickly time fades, not only the pages, but the loves, losses, fears and cares of people's lives.

The Talented Mr Mingella

See the film, *then*, read the book.

Actually, both the book, *The Talented Mr Ripley* by Patricia Highsmith, and the film of the book, directed by Anthony Mingella, are classics of their genre. Though critics might call it a rather low genre.

If you enjoy well-crafted hokum, with precise structures, lush images, clever language and story arcs and deft direction which knows how to pace a story, then the filmed version is definitely recommended. Whilst on its release it received mixed reviews, it could be one of those films that become an 'under the radar' classic, its imperfections only making it more appealing as time goes by.

It's a fact, that I can't watch the movie without thinking of a particular ex-girlfriend (not that our relationship ended with murderous thoughts!), simply because she was the first girlfriend of (as she was perhaps too fond of saying) the film's director, Anthony Mingella. I, now, am perhaps too fond of repeating that, *'I once went out with the first girlfriend of…'*. Such is the power of celebrity (or rather our love of the artists that create works we find compulsive) and Frigyes Karinthy's notion of 'six degrees of separation'. Ripley's equilibrium is certainly shaken and shaped by such matters.

Having just re-watched the movie, for the sixth or seventh time, it dawned on me that I might enjoy reading the book by Patricia Highsmith, on which the film was based.

Often people say book and film *don't* compare. More often than not, people insist the book is better than the film. If a book comes out *after* a film it's, almost certainly, going to be a drag to read. So called 'novelization's' are like reading overweight screenplays, all the excess 'fat' has been put back in. In this case, both book and film are perfect, if what you're looking for is a movie or book about a perfect murderer i.e. one who doesn't get caught.

The plot in the film is marginally more plausible, certainly brisker, and delivers numerous, gentle twists and sharp turns, that don't exist in the book (and these, generally, give the film more colour than Highsmith's deliberately flat prose). I don't know yet, whether the film has taken small bits from the other five books in which Ripley appears and mixed them in, but I would say the director, Anthony Mingella, made with this film, his best film.

The critics, generally, preferred Alain Delon's Ripley, in the previous adaptation, *Purple Noon*, directed by René Clément in 1960 (five years after the book was published). Clément's *Purple Noon* strayed even further from the original novel than Mingella (though, Matt Damon, was quoted as saying, *'I'd like to make the whole film all over again with the same cast and same title but make it completely like the book'*).

Matt Damon's performance was called, by at least one critic, 'weak' but I think this appearance of 'weakness' is actually the actor capturing the facile and hollow nature of Ripley. Ripley, in the end, is not existentially, *simply interesting*, nor is he a question mark, like

Camus' Meursault. Rather, his distanced, squirming, avoidance of self and morality, was created for our pleasure (and also for us to measure ourselves against). Ripley is that flim-flam part of ourselves, the person that performs for others having lost all sense of a core self. Ripley *is* weak.

To read the book (finally!) is also fascinating. The way Highsmith brings the reader into Ripley's mind is a great study on murder, paranoia and the mayhem of such a mind. Of how great weakness mutates, into a murderous, tepid, strength.

The interest we have in Ripley is maintained largely because although he murders you observe (in the book especially) how he has to justify this to himself. He manages to remain an empathetic character (just) but one that is in a state of shock, a willful, uncomprehending shock. The more people he murders, the more opaque his gaze, both internal and external, becomes. It is tragic because it is only in the eyes of the dead, and only momentarily, that he can see his flaw: his narcissism. The tag line to this fiction, is Oscar Wilde's notion, from *The Ballad of Reading Gaol*, 'Every man kills the thing he loves'. In both book and film this idea is conveyed, with a delicious chill, as evil, in its pyrrhic way, triumphs.

Eduardo Niebla

and the Universal Language

I've just been listening to *Mid-week* on BBC Radio 4 with, Eduardo Niebla, a Spanish guitarist, as one of the guests.

It was worth listening to the programme, just to hear him play a little flamenco and speak about his background. He was one of eight children and his parents were from Andalucía though he was born and initially brought up in Tangiers.

This virtuoso musician's description, of both his father and brother, being rather bad at playing the accordion and guitar respectively, was unusual, amusing and sweet. Nonetheless, the real treat was hearing his live rendition of one of his own pieces.

Every now and then, you come across an unknown artist, someone you've never heard of and who you immediately think is fabulous. Niebla, for me, was one of those artists.

Though the truth is, he's been around a long time, has released something like twenty-five albums and in his own country, is not obscure at all.

My 'discovery' reminded me, of the first time I came across Cámaron de la Isla, one of the great flamenco singers of the twentieth century. Cámaron was an amazing singer but also stuck out because he had a 'rock and roll' life style in the arena of classical music.

Cámaron, whose real name was José Monge Cruz, was born in Cádiz, in Andalucía, and like Niebla also came from a family of eight. Both singer and guitarist also share(d) a willingness to mix and fuse their traditional flamenco with sounds from around the world. What struck me most however, during the programme, was just how ignorant I am of 'famous' national figures from other countries.

Music may be a universal language but to prevent it becoming monotone you need to be expansive, travel metaphorically (and literally when you can) and listen, with an open heart, and receptive mind.

That Sleep of Sleeps

Have you ever woken up thinking about the most perfect sleep you ever had? The most refreshing, relaxed, warmth filled, renewing and energizing sleep? The sleep, that far off in the mist of memory, you once had as a child?

It's a bit like that 'kiss of kisses' which for me happened when I was fourteen, at an illicit party. We kissed for what seemed (and might have been) hours. I have long forgotten that girl's name. Even then, I didn't know her well but she and her soft lips, live on, somewhere, deep within the place reserved for the more fragile motes of memory. Like this dam 'sleep of sleeps' which hovers just tangibly in the air of the awoken consciousness. But this 'sleep of sleeps' seems more archetypal, elemental, less visceral and alive than a kiss, it rests more deeply, it is tangential to be sure, an obscure certainty and most definitely hidden.

And, I still desire that sleep. I want so much to

luxuriate in its peaceful valley, wade into the warm waters and soak in depths of utter, sublime unconsciousness. To awake with a passion for the day, limbs fresh, limber, with eyes cracking open, clear and bright. I'm sure I once did that.

I don't mean once. I mean many times. I mean *'Once upon a time...'* and that's right, it is like a story, a long past romance, a tale, a legend of deeds from long ago. It's a myth to me now. A place I know only in my joint ancestral memory, a Jungian subterranean link, a synchronicity but only one *I once lived*. Boy, it would be good to wake up as if I were twelve again. Blood fresh. Fresh as the proverbial daisy, up with the morning lark, bright as the brightest of sayings. Light, as the morning sun, dancing on the windows of the soul.

I'm more like Joe Lampton in *Life at the Top*, though not quite, he's just too bitter, too dark, too much the aging misanthrope. Perhaps Orwell's George Bowling, in *Coming Up For Air*, is closer the mark. George, bald headed and world weary, starts the day locked in the bathroom, kids making a racket outside, wanting to be elsewhere.

No doubt George woke up feeling a bit worn down. He needs to *'come up for air'* like the carp in the pond of Binfield where he once fished as a child. He has been living in the badlands of suburbia and nostalgia too long. He is gasping for the breath, the energy, the sweetness (and perfected slumber) of youth. But the pond has been filled in, the past is a dream and he cannot sleep.

The 'sleep of sleeps' will, no doubt, always, only lightly touch or more probably evade me entirely, that is, until the Big Sleep.

I Don't Believe in Ghosts

I don't believe in ghosts. Do you? I say this, even though once, as a youngster of twelve or thirteen, I woke in the middle of the night to see a small, blond haired boy standing in the corner of my bedroom. I blinked my eyes, didn't want to believe what I was seeing, lay down again, closed my eyes and lay there several moments. When I opened my eyes, and looked again, the spectral figure was still there. At some point, I can't now recall when (disappointingly), the ghost-boy disappeared.

Now, many people (a sister of mine for one), believe that this is the kind of thing that proves the existence of ghosts. Ironically, because I don't see how that follows, numerous 'ghost-believers' have questioned the veracity of my own experience. My vision of a boy, they tell me, must have felt like an hallucination. *'When you see a ghost'*, they say, *'it feels real'*.

Though, in truth, the details of the experience

are now extremely faded, the one thing I do remember, is that it felt exactly, as 'they' say it should have felt, *'real'*.

I think then, their starting point - a propensity to be credulous about ghosts - is what must separate us. The problem, is that when I think about it, I think that how the human mind reproduces the world around us on a daily basis is, in fact, the fantastical and incredible event.

Okay, so occasionally when you're tired, young, scared, drunk, on drugs, excited, bereaved etc. the mind creates an image that doesn't exist in the real, exterior, objective world. So what? We dream every night and our dreams are *not* made from what we'd call hard sense-data i.e. as a result of direct stimuli from the exterior world. Clearly we can produce images without such data. Therefore, a straightforward suggestion is that ghosts are 'created' from a non-external stimulus. Simple really.

The mind is so complex, intricate and extraordinary, why bother to invent the ghost? For entertainment or as imaginative sport? (Certainly writers and filmmakers know how to key into this element of our psyche and enjoy exploiting our primal instinctual fear of 'things that go bump' in the night). To sooth the burning tears of bereavement? For sure, many hold visions of the dead before them (in one way or another) and find it a comfort. Perhaps, just as frequently, it's that people want to believe in other realms and places beyond the reality we know because we just don't have, anthropomorphically satisfying, answers to the metaphysical questions of existence?

Still… ghosts? What do they actually explain? If there is a plane of existence, *beyond* life, what then? The interesting metaphysical question is not whether ghosts exist but why do the creatures that do exist, exist?

The Music of Old Friends

Sad isn't it? How, over the years, we lose touch with friends? Once upon a time, they may have played like a symphony in our heads, adding sound, colour and movement to our lives. But now? Now, we are well past allegro, adagio and scherzo and have moved almost beyond the notes of their finale. Only the finale, in this case, was never very grand, not a place for the wind section to take a deep breath and the strings to pick up their bows.

Rather, with old friends, we note, their music is like the faint whistle of a single pipe or the gentle beat of the bass drum, getting softer and slower (like the heart), until we can barely hear them. These are fanciful metaphors because in real life all your 'former' friends are still dancing on the beach, driving to work, playing with their children (whom you didn't know existed, have never seen or haven't seen 'in an age') and so on.

They are... what? They are carrying on *just like you*. The dying, of their 'music' in your life, is not tragic; it just brings on an occasional moment, a memory, a mood of contemplation; gentle, melancholic silence and perhaps reflections on what made you friends in the first place i.e. their affection and their love. And *'If music be the food of love'* then, as Shakespeare says, well... (beat)... *'play on!'*

A Short Essay into the Body Time

Time is one of our senses.

Look or think of oneself, as a biological creature: a fleshy collection of perceptual apparatus.

What we sense, it seems, deeply influences what we perceive. Physical and chemical interactions, quite literally, colour our perceptions and experiences. Experience for us, by definition, implies duration or passage through time. Passage, that is, as event or series of event. Life, as a line of moments, like strings on a bead. That's what it feels like, our sensation and experience of it. But, of course, there are anomalies produced by memory.

Memory, the faculty which 'holds' or 'captures' time.

Memory is not linear.

One cannot, simply pass a metaphorical finger

along the beads till one finds the right memory. Memory is not strongly chronological. Perhaps, because we hold *all* our memories in the present.

To return, specifically, to time (or time-present) and the analogy of my opening line i.e. time being - or being like - what the senses are like. If heat (for us) is relative, dependent on our own body mass and its condition and the environment. If sight varies, depending on our body's capability (and again) on the external distortions, such as, for example, desert heat making our images of distant objects 'wobble' and so on... Why not the same with time? Why would one expect time to, experientially, feel stable, static, regular? The interface, between body and world, is a roller-coaster of sensation. Experience, a bungee jump of sensation, collated, stamped, impressed and put in the album, of memory.

However, time we should like to say, as with the other senses, is a supplier of information (a wealth of it). It's our filter, our interface, our horizon, of what *is*. Part, in fact, of what 'is-ness' is for us.

If you have no memory, what is time? If each moment, is the *only* moment, does time stop? Also, surely changes in perception alter experience? A fly, a worm, an amoeba, a tree etc., these other living sensuous (and non-sensuous) organisms certainly perceive, and/or respond differently to existence, due to their different embodiment. Perhaps, time is the type of *body,* you are constituted of? Perhaps, the universe, the oneness, is somehow static, motionless, ever present, ever the same and it is merely us, the divided, the fragmentary, the momentary being, that senses change and time.

Gnostics once said we are fragments, shards, from a broken universe-jug or splinters, of the One. Hume says, we 'fill-in' *cause,* push it *into* experience - event following event - when it's not *there*, we reify. Perhaps, that is what time is like? And, we push it into *(onto, at)* a world, which is timeless?

If we heard everything all in the same moment, every sound in the universe, what would sound be? What is sight, when physics tells us, that we see 'dead' stars? So, in a now-of-no-time or rather a now-of-all-time surely we would be unplaced, un-bodied and time would be dead?

If we had a view from nowhere. If there were no subject/object divide. If we could cleanse the doors of perception and see everything as it is, infinite. If infinity was somehow - language fails here – 'contained'? The borders and the limits of time, would surely cease? Time is a relative: event A, event B, event C and so on, *not* the ABC of eternal now-ness, oneness, unity.

Iris Murdoch said everywhere we humans see parts but intuit wholes. Perhaps, true perception, is *not-perception*: a loss of seeing parts and *intuiting* wholes. Existentialists talk of a leap into the abyss. Perhaps, this is *loss of self*, from part to whole, from fragment to jug, from time to non-time, from being to eternal no-thing-ness? Perhaps body-time is *not* all there is? Perhaps body-time is *not*.

A Disembodied Aesthetic of Jack Kerouac

There's a point in Jack Kerouac's *On the Road*: he's not been travelling for that long but he wakes up in a strange motel room not knowing who he is. That is, it takes him a few minutes to come to a recognition, as to who he is and where he is.

It's not like 'a lacking', a doziness, a morning drowsiness, that *loss of self*. It's closer to the true self than anything else we ever discover, uncover or recover. We *find*, we have thoughts, things flow *through* us.

Most of the time, we barely even consider why or where the thoughts have come from, except to say *'I thought…'* this or that. That's why reading has such a peculiarly strong pull on us. Why should it draw us so, thought in ink? We reflect, absorb and create, we play, we doze, we imagine, we are transported, to *'far off places'* they say. But, all places from the page, are far off, all surreal in their existence. Why? Because

218

we have to translate from another mind, transpose the inner of them made exterior, to the inner of us. That is a peculiarity, a specificatory element of humanity: story, word, thought, language. It makes us human through the generations.

But so… this self, this *Who-am-I?*-asker, is already cloudy in their question. Far from the place of answer. Why… how even, can one ask, who oneself is? The question is full of paradox. You, the speaker, ask who you, the speaker, is? Are you the voice of the question or are you the source of the voice of the question (or are you beyond any voice)?

I will not go on too much about the *'being of the being'*, as Heidegger might put it. I get lost, I think, in the being of my being, being the being, beyond which I have being but *am* or perhaps *am not*. It is beautiful, in its meditative, transcendentalism, his work; his mind. But it's outside of me.

His words, circle like eddies in a whirlpool, round and round and back again. They cannibalize each other, each thought, tracks back and loses itself (and you) back in and on itself. Its better... no, it helps, to pause, and try to think *within* one's own thoughts, feeble as one might feel them to be.

But, they can't be febrile, because in the end they will tap into, and contribute to, the inner sanctum of the eons old mind that all of us maintain. The Akasic Record, the record of every human thought (written on the wind) is recorded too, within our being. The Jungian archetype is me and it is you.

The poetry of being is a thing, inexplicable, to words. It is ineffable, unutterable. Words cannot explain, what it is to see a herd of deer, unexpectedly, cross your path, whilst walking in the forest. The path of your life, led to this vision, the immensity of chance, fate, material force, brought you before the deer but that cross-flowing of innumerable coincidences (of infinite past) that reaches beyond (not only) you; all that, can only be described, a hint upon the breath.

Word ignites visions you have seen, with those unseen. It reaches beyond the terrestrial. Logos has long been *a* god (part of a lower pantheon) but now it is a secular god in its own right. Though truly speaking (writing), I think all gods are dead, not just the one singular *God*, as Nietzsche decreed. Seers and oracles are no more; higher beliefs void; prayer silent. The mystical higher self, is here, it is you. Nothing more is needed, the only philosopher alive is you. Not in solipsistic oneness, there is 'other' beyond the eye, it's just, I think, that all being is equally powerful. Not though, masterful.

There are all kinds of masters and slaves, all kinds of thesis, antithesis and synthesis. All manner of subject and subjugation. But being, is *mode* beyond control, infinite in its existence, outside of time. This is not belief, some kind of faith, it is seen and so it *is*. It *is* and so it is seen.

Proof is not the body I have, (and truthfully) I just wonder if this is how it is. But I relate to that *loss of self*, have experienced it, and have had conversations with others about it. A good friend of mine, just the other day, said late at night, she realized nothing 'held her up'. Her existence was, as if it were, air, a light nothingness, a puff of cigarette smoke, twisting like a dancer to no tune. For moments together, she had the feeling that all her thoughts, all her disquisitions on Life, Art, Love, Politics, Food, Home, the Universe or whatever and whatnever, meant nothing. Everything was, as fragile and fleeting, as mist on glass, touching and not touching a hard reality.

It touched her like a spectre, at least for a moment, she was afeard, frightened by its immateriality, its lack of it-ness, *her* lack of it-ness that is.

These moments of the abyss we do not live in. We exist, but we do not live. Like the dark, pallid vision, of the inner self of a zombie, we are undead, unlife. It's as if we are floating in the infinite, the cosmos of void, we are filled with 'without-ness'. But it is a twilight, an inner being holds us, pulls us back but we understand that being does not belong to us or rather we do not own it, it just *is* (without word, without explanation). Is-ness *is*. As Wittgenstein lamented, of that which we cannot speak of, let us be silent. Some, take this to mean *beyond* what we can speak of, is meaningless. Others (including Wittgenstein), that only meaning exists, beyond our silence.

But we live with spectres, of one sort or another, all the time. The *'What will I do?'*, the *'Am I doing this right?'*, the *'What have I done?'* and the *'I wish I could'*. In fact, mostly, we mix a little of all of them together, in every thought and gesture. The fear of finding nothing at the bottom of our well, drives most of us, either to keep digging ever deeper or to dig more wells, and yet more wells, as, very consciously, a distraction. We thirst. The problem of existing *is*, we thirst for the emptiness of being, and return to being, only to thirst again. We can be every-day, every day, but every day we know that every day, is more than every-day-ness.

Why? Because you cannot, as Heraclitus said, step into the same river twice: as you eat, the apple rots; as you sleep, the body ages; as you look, the cloud rolls. Can you hear the music or just one note at a time? Events, as Humean bundles, trundle past, and time is just a construct of our Kantian minds: we make cause, fill 'event' with meaning; beyond the phenomena, we hope, the noumena.

But probably, we know as much as tree, leaf, twig, foot, ant, brick, nose, pike, felt-tip, gooseberry, angel, rhino, lampshade, dog, kneecap, tooth, elephant, rocket, lettuce. We are, as knowing as glass, as dark as pitch; words spill from us, like light from the sun, but not much is illuminated, not much of what *is*.

Being is not good or bad, living is. Do you *own* empires Adolf? Genghis? Nero? Is the cosmos yours Buddha? Christ? Muhammad? Is the sun conscious? The sea alive? The air delighted? The ground, a holiness, that smiles? Can you measure happiness, record a void, scale a vanished mountain, saddle unicorns? These are dreams that illuminate nothing much but occupy us, entertain us, in our existence.

Jack captures this sense of things; it reads well, I think.

Therefore I Am

Digging around my old junk, I found this on a scrap of paper, in a hand I didn't recognize. Was it something I once wrote?

What you read is a lie. I do not exist. This page is invisible. All lies, lie here. All words die on the tongue. They were never written. Never spoken. Never thought. I do not exist. I never was. I never died because you never read these lines and I never lived in you. You never were. You're not here. You do not exist. You are a figment, a corner, around which I do not turn. Skin, I cannot taste. Breath, I cannot see. Eyes, I cannot touch. Teeth, I cannot smell. Thought, I cannot hear. You exist to nobody. No-one. No thing. You are nothing. You don't understand.

You, do not exist, therefore, I am.

Praise for other books

PLAYING MACBETH

'Just plain excellent'

*****Five Stars Amazon-Audible

'Insightful, entertaining, a lesson in process of any kind, really honest assessments, beautiful language, authentic alive reading by author. Loved it'

'Fantastic insider's account... the author has a splendid voice which enhances the experience. If I did have a complaint it would only be that I was sorry for it to end so soon… I would recommend this book to anyone who loves the language of Shakespeare...' Amazon-Audible customer, USA

'Fascinating autobiographical effort to pass on the very essence of the art of theatrical performance to the next generation of actors... a thrilling journey... monumental... it's essential reading for any actor.'

*****Five Star rating Readers' Favorite

*****Five Star rating Barnes and Noble

THE LAST DAYS OF ADAM

'Extremely well written, allowing us to identify with the world of the Judenrat and the Jews during WWII, and it engages us well in moral questions... Excellent... unites the historical with the emotional.'

*****Five Star rating Readers' Favorite

THE STONES OF MITHRAS

'What I enjoyed most about this collection was that it discussed a unique topic. There aren't many poetry collections out there that discuss architecture and ancient societies the way that Tim Dalgleish does... thoughtful, mysterious and a very good read. ... I was very impressed... I look forward to seeing more of what this author publishes in the future.'

*****Four Star rating Readers' Favorite

ABOUT THE AUTHOR

Tim Dalgleish is the author of two volumes of poetry *The Stones of Mithras* and *Penumbra*, numerous plays and a book on acting called *Playing Macbeth: An Actor's Journey into the Role*. As an actor he has worked with theatre companies from RAT Theatre to Voices of the Holocaust. He played Snout in *A Midsummer Night's Dream* as part of the RSC's Open Stages programme and was the lead in *Macbeth* for the Open Theatre Group. He has appeared briefly in several feature films, the most recent being *Finding Fatimah* (with Danny Ashok and Nina Wadia), the British gangster movie *Milk and Honey* (with Mark Wingett) and was also in the short film *Imagine* which received Special Mention at the Marbella International Film Festival. His book *Playing Macbeth* was called by reviewers *'A thrilling journey'*, *'Monumental'* and a *'Fantastic insider's view'*. He regularly narrates audio books, the latest being: *Exit Stage Left* by Adam Croft and *After Dunkirk: D-Day and How We Planned the Second Front* by Major John Dalgleish (his great uncle). More information at www.lookingfortim.com.

Printed in Great Britain
by Amazon